Struggles of Strangers

Struggles of Strangers
OF BONDING AND FREEDOM

Junis Sultan

© 2017 Junis Sultan
All rights reserved.

ISBN: 1542416787
ISBN 13: 9781542416788

Acknowledgements

Heartfelt thanks to
Joan Herrick and *Brenda Clark,* my faithful friends. Your empathic assistance during the revisions have helped me get hold of deep thoughts and emotions.
Irena Praitis, my committed writing teacher. Your poignant remarks and questions have helped me shape this memoir.
the *Gotham Writers Workshop.* You provided a safe place for my memoir to grow.
Nicole Bailey, who kindly helped me revise the first draft.
Alexandra Eryiğit-Klos, my eagerly interested and supportive editor.
Erhan Dogan, who greatly supported and produced the book cover and the book trailer.
the *Media Kanzlei Frankfurt.* You provided expertise and friendly advice.

Peggy Preciado, my first writing teacher. You detected the value of my family's story and encouraged me to keep writing.

my dear parents, who provided many information about our family history. You faced many challenges in your life and yet kept fighting for us. You deserve all the happiness and peace.

*To the faithful,
to the young,
and to the curious who want to create more
happiness and peace*

Some names, places, and identifying details have been changed to protect the privacy of individuals.

Table of contents

Prologue xiii

I. Mosul	August 1986-January 1991 1	
II. In the Air And on the Road	January-October 1991 27	
III. Kastel	November 1991-March 1992 73	
	March 1992-August 1993 89	
	September 1993-August 1997 107	
	September 1997-August 2003 129	
	September 2003-June 2006 189	
	July 2006-October 2007 235	
	October 2007-December 2008 243	
IV. Liederbach	January 2009-August 2010 253	
V. Fullerton	August 2010-April 2011 267	
VI. Kastel	April 2011-May 2011 289	
VII. Liederbach	June 2011-November 2011 307	

Epilogue 317

Prologue

"And then came the bloody bastard"

Junis Sultan

GROWING UP, I OFTEN WONDERED whether my skin looks brown or white. My hair is certainly black, and my eyes are brown. Many "Westerners" I met imagined "the Middle East" when they saw me or heard my name—*Junis Sultan*. Many were surprised that I spoke their language accent-free. "Middle Easterners," in contrast, were repeatedly disappointed that I did not speak Arabic fluently. It was often confusing for people, including myself, to categorize me.

My story is of unexpected fate and reinvention. In 1991, after surviving the Gulf War, my family moved from Iraq to Germany. I was 4 years old at the time. One of my early memories is of watching the television news with my father. He raised his finger and shouted, "The West imposed those bloody sanctions on Iraq, not Saddam[1]." Intimidated by his anger, I asked him what he meant. He said, "The West is Europe, North America, and Australia. They've killed millions and now they kill us." I felt warned. When I attended kindergarten in 1992, I experienced, however, that the warning to beware all "Westerners" proved wrong. In fact, we did live together in peace—at least for some years.

Since those early days, I've strived to live in harmony with people who celebrated "the Middle East," or "the West." And even though I've repeatedly failed, sometimes in regrettably destructive ways, I've kept trying to satisfy and balance our

---

[1] Saddam Hussein (4/28/1937 - 12/30/2006), fifth President of Iraq, serving from 7/16/1979 to 4/9/2003

common needs. *What is "the Middle East" or "the West" anyway?* I wondered time and time again.

The cultural divisiveness among us always seemed constructed, often destructive, and thus wrong to me. Growing up in Germany, I often pondered about the true meaning of our existence. *Were we not in truth all born as precious social individuals, connected and meant to support each other while realizing our personal dreams? How else could we be safe, happy, and at peace?*

Still, I frequently doubted our connectedness, especially when meeting other people. Many "Westerners" confronted me with their imagined knowledge of me, "Does your mother wear a hijab?" "Were your sisters' marriages arranged?" "Do you hate Jews? The United States?" To their surprise, none of it applied to me. I often felt taken aback and wondered how they could apply their negative images of "the Middle East" without knowing me first. "Middle Easterners," then again, were often disappointed by me as well, "Don't do this! It's haram." I often felt like strange, disconnected person after those interactions.

The thousands-of-years old stories of my name have shaped my complex identity. In 1993, during my first school year, my father told me that Junis derives from *Yunus,* "an important prophet in the Quran who strongly believed in God's rules." In a Catholic religion class, I learned that the Hebrew Bible and the New Testament first told the story of Yunus under the name of *Jonah.* "Jonah means dove in

Hebrew, and a dove is a symbol of peace," my teacher said before she read out, "Jonah was ordered by God to go to Nineveh and prophesy against the people's great wickedness. Afraid, however, that God would simply forgive the sinners, he boarded a ship that sailed in the opposite direction. When God created a storm at sea because of his disobedience, the sailors found Jonah responsible and threw him overboard. Still, Jonah was lucky since he was swallowed by a whale. Inside, he repented, thanked God for his mercy, and committed himself to God's will. Eventually, the whale spewed him out. He went to Nineveh and convinced the people to heed his prophecies. Nevertheless, he still struggled to understand God's forgiveness." I was looking at my teacher with large, fascinated eyes. While I had no idea what was waiting for me in life, I knew that I wanted to have a relationship with God, too. Moreover, *I, too, wanted to be lifted up when I fell.*

My first name, Junis, often caused insecurities among people. *Jonas,* the Greek version of Jonah, has become a popular name in Germany since the 1990s. That is probably why many Germans called me Jonas after I had introduced myself; sometimes, even when I spelled out, "J U N I S." *Did they ignore my real name with intent?* I wondered time and again. Some asked with lowered eyebrows to spell it out again. Often, their second response was, "Where does that name come from?" The problem started when I was naturalized in 1991. "Younes is its international notation, but it would complicate matters for Germans. They're not used to 'Y.' 'Y' is only used in few words in German," a public official told my mother. My first name thus was Germanized. I was too young to notice the forced assimilation. Yet, many "Middle Easterners" did from the beginning. "So are you a real Arab?" many asked after reading my name. Usually, I told them where my parents were born to explain how my name was Germanized—which often led to an awkward silence. Growing up in Germany, I increasingly asked myself, *Does the spelling of my name really define who I am?*

My last name, Sultan, repeatedly raised fear or false idolization. *Sultan* originally meant "strength" in Arabic. Over time, it also became a title for leaders that claimed independence of any higher ruler. According to Wikipedia—the world's leading online encyclopedia, launched in "the West"—one of the most famous sultans is *Mehmed II* who conquered Constantinople and ended the 1000-year-long Byzantine Empire in 1453. I assume his destructive power made him famous in "the West," which—as *Edward Said*[2] would say—has strived to invent itself as good in direct contrast to their imagined evil Orient. Strangely, my father ascribed the exact opposite value to "the Middle East." *As if Mehmed II were better than any murderer. And as if killing 4,000 non-Muslims in 1453 were good.* I often struggled to understand why people demonized or idolized other human beings. *Were we not all more or less flawed and yet worthy?*

---

2 Edward Wadie Said (11/1/1935 - 09/25/2003), professor of literature, public intellectual, and founder of the academic field of postcolonial studies, known for the book Orientalism (1978)

In my school days in Germany between 1993 and 2006, I was mostly taught about the merits of "the West." We investigated the European Enlightenment of the 17th and 18th century. *Kant's*[3] "categorical imperative"—to "act only according to that maxim whereby one can will that it should become a universal law"—seemed to me like a precious idea that would bring peace among people. We read the classics of the German literary periods of which the 18th century Storm und Stress period was my favorite since it allowed the free expression of strong emotions. I excitedly examined the revolutions for values like freedom and unity: 1776 in America, 1789 in France, and 1848 in Germany.

Above all, I embraced the 1948 Universal Declaration of Human Rights (UDHR), the first document I read at school that was drafted by an international committee and that aimed for peace for all people—a dream I wished everybody shared.

While our teachers claimed that the unprecedented horrors of World War II led to the UDHR, I learned in 2009 in a rare seminar on "post-colonialism" at Goethe University that Nazi Germany was not a short-term mistake though, which killed more than 50 million people around the globe, but a result of the repeatedly propagandistic and bloody history of "the West." Like *Hannah Arendt*[4] said, European nationalisms

---

[3] Immanuel Kant (04/22/1724 - 02/12/1804), German philosopher who is considered a central figure in modern philosophy

[4] Johanna "Hannah" Arendt (10/14/1906 - 12/04/1975), German-born Jewish American political theorist

and colonialisms blended with post-enlightenment racial theories in the 18th and 19th century. European, male philosophers like *Locke, Montesquieu, Hume,* and Kant claimed the natural superiority of the white race and thus paved the way for a pseudo-legitimized enslavement and killing of non-white people centuries before *Hitler*. Moreover, our seminar discussions opened my eyes to the subtle ways of how similar mass killings continued in the 21st century. Still, one burning question remained, *How could we overcome these injustices?*

I was eager to find out. From 2010 to 2011, I studied political science at California State University, Fullerton. Since "J" is an affricate in English and not a semi-vowel like in German, I anticipated awkward situations. Indeed, many Americans struggled to pronounce "Junis" correctly, even after I had told them the proper pronunciation. Sometimes, when I was tired of repeatedly repeating myself, I just smiled friendly and let them believe my name was Junis instead of Younes, what it should have been. I understood their problem. Like in Germany, many "Westerners" changed my name to deal with it more easily. *They didn't necessarily intend to assimilate me,* I sensed. *More often than not, they simply struggled to learn something new.*

During my political philosophy course, I read and learned about the Greek, the Hebrew, the Roman, and the Christian societies, which my senior professor called "the foundational stories of the West." In particular, I enjoyed our recurring discussions about whether we could know truths about ethics—right individual conduct—and politics—right collective life. I, like a couple of my fellow students, believed we could.

At the end of the semester, my professor suggested that modern, 21st century's global liberalism represented the synthesis of all stories of "the West." Skeptical of his Eurocentric perspective, I asked him about the role of the rest of the world. He pondered for a second before he raised his head and said with a raised eyebrow, "Well, there was Mesopotamia, Egypt, Persia, and then came the bloody bastard Mohammed who spread Islam by the sword." Sitting in the last row, I looked at him with big eyes. *As if the stories of "the West" were free of bloodshed.* I remained silent and waited to hear more about what he thought; but he stopped himself. "Oh, shit, is she here? The one with the scarf?" he asked, looking around.

Her name was *Manar,* which means "guiding light" in Arabic. She did not attend our class that day, but I did—embodying a vibrant blend of Judeo-Christian-Muslim, German, Arabic, and Ottoman traditions. That day, like so many times before, I wondered, *How could we overcome hostile attitudes and create more happiness and peace among each other and within ourselves?*

I. Mosul

August 1986-January 1991

"Freestyle, chest-high"

Junis Sultan

Sunday, August 31, 1986, around noon

Fiery fierceness intruded into the room from the outside and besieged my parents and me with a breath-scorching late-summer heat. The air conditioner had been sent out for repair. It left a rectangular hole in the wall. Off and on, a hammering, grinding noise broke through the sidewall. The hospital at the Tigris River was under renovation.

My father bent over my mother to kiss her sweaty forehead. She was lying on a rusty metal bed, holding me in her arms and breastfeeding me. She had lost a lot of blood during the delivery. Her light skin looked almost white, like some strands of her shoulder-length hair that had lost its dark pigments in the previous years. She was 42 years old.

"We should give him a name that's easy to pronounce for people in Germany," she said. Understanding, my father nodded. He gently kissed my cheek before he walked to the hole in the wall. "Look, one can see Nabi Yunus from here!" he pointed outside, looking at the white mosque on the hill of the Nineveh ruins where the Prophet Jonah is believed to be buried. An octagonal minaret ascended to the light-blue sky. From her bed, she could see its white spire. She had visited the ancient mosque before and was still impressed by its beauty. "Why don't we call him Younes?" he said. She looked over him, thinking over his proposal. He wore no moustache, which was unusual for Iraqi men. His white shirt was damp; the sweat was gleaming on his brown skin. He looked younger than 47 years old. Suddenly, she turned to me, smiling. She liked the name. "From this day on, you are Younes," she said.

Outside, direct sunbeams seared every blade of grass, except for those at the close by Tigris River. The turquoise water, calm and shallow, could almost be crossed by foot that season. From October to May, however, it would rise to 200 yards width and depth and majestically run through metropolitan space, which was inhabited by 600,000 people.

His look lingered on the riverside miracles. Dark green palm leaves waved in a breeze from time to time. Red grapes and pomegranates thrived nearby as well as green apples, pears, figs, and heavy watermelons. Full-fleshed tomatoes, eggplants, okra pods, and cucumbers flourished at the water's edge, where green soft-shell turtles jumped into the water from time to time while swarms of black-and-white lapwings were sitting on tall poplars, calling, full of life.

The Tigris was Mosul's source of life. As a young boy, my father spent hours playing in the river with his friends from Shifa—a poor district of Mosul. Often, black river buffaloes joined them to cool off in the water while their farmers slept on deck chairs. Sometimes, the river was so crowded that he and his friends had no place to move. Some buffaloes would let them lie on their backs for a while, but most would resist. Some would eat aquatic plants, and some would let their feces in the water. Nature served everyone sufficiently. When he and his friends were hungry, they would pick a watermelon, eat it, and jump back into the water.

Despite or maybe because of his simple beginnings, he reached for the stars from early on. He was born on April 12, 1939. From 1947 to 1956, he attended public school in Mosul. During that time, his family shared one room for eating, talking, crying, and loving. Still, he was privileged since he had his own table for his studies, while the rest of the 250 square feet had to serve for everyone during the nights when all laid closely together. His parents wished for at least one of their six children to have a chance to study and see the world. In the daytime, his oldest sister thus helped him prepare for exams while the other family members worked for the family bread bakery. His mother supervised the production, his father the selling. At that time, 14,000 soldiers were stationed in Mosul, and since his father, a World War I veteran, knew some of them, most of the bread was sold to the military base. In spring 1956, the family finally received the joyful news that my father's excellent graduation grades qualified him for a full study abroad scholarship.

He studied mechanical engineering at the University of Wales from 1957 to 1962. In the winter of 1960, he went to a dance in the Student Union, a plain building with wooden chairs lining a gray wall. He was waiting for a soda at the bar when *Gabriela,* a fellow student, approached him with her new friend. While Gabriela introduced him to the young lady, who had come from Germany as an au pair to improve her English, someone dropped a coin in the jukebox. Shortly, romantic strings filled the room with *Maurice Chevalier's* "Gigi.[5]" A young man popped up and led Gabriela to the dance floor, where dozens of couples found themselves in a close embrace. Even though first quiet and hesitant, my father soon dared to ask the new young lady, who would later become my mother, if she would like to dance. Barely

---

5 title song of the 1958 American musical-romance film "Gigi," which portrayed how love overcomes cynicism

17 years old, she blushed, but eventually allowed herself to say, "Yes." Both were visibly attracted by each other's courteous behavior. Smiling, they entered the dance floor.

In the next three months, they met occasionally on campus. First, they just had coffee together, but soon they arranged to meet more frequently. One day, he wrote an article for the university newspaper about a campus exhibition. He had taken a picture of her and put it on the title page. When she thanked him the next day, half-embarrassed and half-delighted, he invited her to his apartment for dinner. Soon, she visited him more often. They would cook together, listen to music, twist and dance, and also do the housework together. She knew how much he had to study.

In the summer of 1961, she had to go back to Germany to graduate from high school. At their final meeting at the railway station, both confessed that they would miss each other a lot.

When they hugged each other, tears began to roll down their cheeks. Suddenly, they felt they were in love. *They were too conservative, too young to comment on it.* His mother used to tell him that having a girlfriend without getting married first was a sin, and he used to listen to her. My mother, a cat friend and hobby soccer player, had no experience at all in love relationships. Still, both sensed that their separation would be too painful to bear.

While he stayed in England to continue his studies, they told each other in many letters about their sore unhappiness, "We can't let more days pass by and be separated. We need to find a way to come together again." Yet, distance and time became even bigger. In spring 1962, after he had graduated with a Bachelor of Science degree with honors, he returned to Mosul to attend the obligatory 12-month military academy. Their love was asking for bold action.

On July 30, 1963, a Tuesday, she made a life-changing decision against the wish of her parents, who were skeptical about the chances of an intercultural marriage with an Iraqi. While they vacationed in Yugoslavia, she took a train to Frankfurt, where she boarded a propeller-driven plane that flew 2,700 miles south-east—to Baghdad. By late evening, my father received a telegram from *Stanley,* an Iraqi Airways pilot. "We've got a young German woman who is asking for you. She can stay the night at our place. Please, pick her up tomorrow."

The very next day at dawn, he drove 250 miles south. They met at the airport and hugged each other with tears of joy. The first night, they stayed at *Nuri's,* his brother's place in central Baghdad.

On August 1, 1963, a Thursday morning, they took a bus to the register's office in casual clothes to swear their love to a public official who declared them husband and wife.

Still, it would take some years until things worked out all well for them. After their civil marriage, they drove to Mosul to meet the rest of the family in their new home, which my father had built with his first salaries. They were welcomed with words and kisses, and even though he translated everything into English, she felt completely insecure. She did not know much about Iraqi culture. She didn't know what to expect from others and how to behave. She wondered if she would be accepted.

Shortly after tea, her uncertainty turned into a personal trauma. Since it quickly got around that "a woman from Europe had joined the family," dozens of relatives came over to see her. Many females looked over her from head to toe. "Why did you pick a European? We have many good women waiting for you here," they told him. He did not translate their words, but she understood their jealous looks and mocking laughter. He did, too. However, he did not dare to criticize his relatives since he knew it would have been considered treacherous. Not knowing what to do, he led her to her room upstairs, where she broke down in tears of sorrow. She felt utterly lonely and helpless. She spoke neither Arabic, nor did she have anyone who would defend her.

In the following weeks, she spent many desperate hours alone in her room, lying on her bed underneath a running ceiling fan, feeling lonely, crying, being eaten by mosquitoes and sweating while facing a heat she had never known before. He, on the other side, was working in an electricity generating company all day every day except Friday, the weekly holiday.

Fortunately, the picture changed for the better after half a year when he started a new job in the field of power generation. Since he earned more money, they moved out and rented their own house. My mother made new friends and started learning Arabic. In 1966, *Manal,* their first child, was born. In 1969, *Malik,* their second child. In the 1970s, my father worked on various projects, such as establishing three textile factories in Mosul. When she was pregnant with *Nour* in 1972, he attended a four-month management course in Sweden. Soon after his return, he became the General Director of the three Mosul textile factories. His career as an outstanding manager and popular figure of the Ministry of Industry began. In 1979 and in 1982, *Mamun* and *Alim* were born. In that period, he developed a plan to expand the Iraqi textile industry. By 1986, businesspersons and ministers from around the world were inviting him for meetings in exclusive hotels and federal headquarters around the globe to finalize the economic future for millions of people.

As fortune wanted it, I was born into a high society family.

WEDNESDAY, SEPTEMBER 3, 1986

Three days after the delivery, *Salim,* our private chauffeur, picked up my mother and me to bring us home. We left the hospital under bright sunlight and got into the new, black SUV that was parked at the main entrance. He drove us to the Mansur district of South-West Mosul, close to the industrial area. Shortly after he had stopped next to a high sandstone brick wall, a security person in a white cabin opened the electric gate in front of us. We entered the city-like site. A factory with arched roofs was visible in the distance. We drove toward it on an ascending street, passing family homes, a kindergarten, a school, and several shops before we stopped at the last right bend next to a huge and well-maintained property—a flat-roofed, two-story mansion. Its facade was clad with hand-chiseled sandstones. On each story, wide floor windows led to four large balconies. A prefabricated pathway led to the center of the building, a two-story entrance hall that was accessed through an extra-tall arched front door. Next to the pathway, sprinklers were watering the neatly cut front lawn, where two trimmed palm trees had grandly risen into the sky.

While an electronic gate opened to our left, Salim slowly entered the property. He parked on a long, paved gateway. "We're home," he said peacefully before he opened the passenger door for my mother. She thanked him, "Shukran jazilan," and got out of the car.

Carrying me on her arm, she slowly walked behind our house. As she entered the backyard, an excited clucking broke out. Dozens of chickens began to run around in the mesh wire enclosure on our left. She grinned at them before she crossed our soccer-field-sized lawn, heading toward our multi-colored rosarium. Most flowers in our garden were roses. They blossomed wonderfully. Despite her post-childbirth pain, she bent down to smell the roses' sweet flavor. Breathing deeply through her nose, she smiled again. She loved our garden. She loved nature.

Sadiq, our private gardener, saw us and approached us from the two-bedroom bungalow that had been built for our employees in the far left corner of our property.

"As-salāmu 'alaykum.[6] Who did you bring?" he asked with a smile.

"This is Younes," she said, smiling back.

"Masha'Allah![7] Ahlan wa sahlan Younes!" he welcomed me.

He turned on the garden hose to refill our turquoise-tiled swimming pool with fresh water. Behind our pool, a ten-foot sandstone brick wall marked off one textile factory my father led.

Since the production depended on clean water, my father had financed the building of new waterworks in Mansur. They also delivered water to other residential areas of Mosul. He enjoyed being helpful. Giving back to the people was a question of justice for him. He knew about the limiting effects poverty could have on a family from his own childhood and thus even financed the building of 2,000 family homes, some schools, kindergartens, and shops with the profits he generated.

---

6 greeting in Arabic, means "peace be upon you"

7 Arabic phrase, means "God has willed," expresses appreciation, joy, praise, or thankfulness for an event or person that was just mentioned

While the water was running, my mother thanked Sadiq for his work and excused herself.

She walked back to our house and entered through an aluminum French door our living hall. Thick, red curtains behind tall, arched windows darkened the cool room. Ornate carpets covered parts of the light, natural stone floor. Two golden chandeliers were shining from the high ceiling.

Before she could walk to our kitchen, my siblings came running to hug her. "Mama, you are back!" they shouted excitedly. A beaming smile graced her face. She had never imagined living such a life blessed with so many children after her initial struggles in Mosul.

Winter 1987

Saddam Hussein indulged public officials, like my father, who worked in the Ministry of Industry, in many ways to keep them quiet and loyal to his authoritarian rule. Every year, we were given a piece of land from the government free. On a monthly basis, we received plenty of food free, such as bags of beans, rice, and flour, and boxes with fresh eggs and meat. In addition, we obtained, for a tenth of the market price, house appliances, such as air-conditioners, and other items, such as hand-knotted carpets and designer furniture. Many Iraqis, in contrast, often had to wait months before they could buy these items, while certain goods were only reserved for the high society—people like us. My mother, helpful as she was, usually distributed the things we received among our relatives and our neighbors, knowing that we would never lack anything.

In winter 1987, a middle-aged man delivered a packet four times my height. He left it in our kitchen in the morning. We waited for my father, who came home from work at night, to open the box of a modern, U.S. refrigerator with an ice maker that would provide cubed filtered ice, one of the things only people like us received. Actually, we had already obtained two excellent refrigerators.

As a result of material abundance, our basement was a vast warehouse. We even had two basements since we possessed another 7,400-square-foot property in the Yarmouk district of western Mosul. Salim shuttled us between our houses every day to make sure we did not miss anything. As an infant, I was too young to understand how spoiled we were.

My father did not discuss politics to avoid getting in trouble with Saddam Hussein's all-controlling and oppressive regime. August 1984, however, was an exception. Saddam Hussein invited him for a talk because, for the third year in a row, he had been nominated by the Ministry of Industry as "Manager of the Year."

The nomination was based on various categories, such as productivity and labor conditions. The first textile factory of Mosul started with 400 workers in 1954. When my father took over as manager, he disposed of all the old machines and bought (with a state loan) expensive, computer-controlled sewing and weaving machines from Europe. Since he increased the productivity and profit rate tremendously, he was able to hire new workers and even build two new factories in the 1980s. By 1987, more than 7,000 people worked in the five textile factories he led. The workers held shares of the company and received regular and advanced training as well as retirement income and health insurance by the company free—another new concept he introduced.

When he met Saddam Hussein in his palace in Baghdad in 1984, he behaved naively confident. Most Iraqis did not dare to look Saddam Hussein in his eyes since it could have been judged as disrespect, which could have led to unpredictable and probably serious consequences. Still, my father decided to be self-assured and positive about creating new opportunities for Iraq's economy. He thus did look Saddam Hussein in the eyes while they shook hands in an extremely intense and silent moment that was telecasted on state television. In the following two-hour interview, which took place at a round table with other key politicians, Saddam Hussein talked about Iraq's economy and politics, surprisingly, in liberal terms as if he was not a dictator anymore. Moreover, when my father dared to argue in favor of a market economy, Saddam Hussein, for the first time, publicly advocated it even though he had considered himself a socialist. My father felt extraordinarily proud about his achievements and, like many other Iraqis, hopeful with regard to Iraq's economic development.

It was not the first or the last time my father appeared on state television. Editors of women's magazines interviewed him frequently since they were interested in the company's pro-woman concept. 6,000 of his workers and three of his seven top managers were women. The televised interviews usually took place in his office. He would be sitting at his teakwood table, wearing the finest suits and having his short, wiry, black hair combed aside while he would be listening and answering questions with a focused and determined face, weighing and striving for excellence.

After 1984, the picture in his office behind his desk showed him and Saddam Hussein shaking hands. It hung next to the regular picture of Saddam Hussein in uniform that was present all over the country. It counted as an exceptional social status in Iraq to be in a picture with Saddam Hussein—shaking hands.

A Thursday during the summer of 1988

While abundance and prestige surrounded me as a barely 2-year-old child, one of the things I enjoyed most was exploring our endless garden in Mansur. Lush fig, apple, orange, lemon, and pear trees grew along our rear sandstone brick wall. With the colorful sea of roses, *our garden smelled so endearingly sweet.* I easily spent hours outside, running, smelling, smiling.

When Sadiq picked and washed our vegetables in the morning, I often imitated him. Around 11 a.m., we would sit down at the kitchen table in the bungalow, side by side, and eat cucumbers and chilies from one plate. Sadiq came from a suburb of Mosul. He had white hair and a wrinkly face. He was hard of hearing, and since I did not talk much, we got along perfectly. Sadiq was a calm and grateful person.

On Thursdays my mother brought him a carton of Marlboros for less than 2 U.S. dollars from the market downtown where only public officials could shop. She regularly bought rare items from that market for our relatives and friends. Sadiq's smile, however, was the biggest when she returned from the market. I loved his smile.

Saturday, August 6, 1988

On August 6, 1988, my mother left our house in the morning with our new Toyota to do the last-minute shopping for our upcoming vacation. She was wearing oversized, black sunglasses and a tailored, black dress, looking like *Audrey Hepburn*[8], as her friends often said.

We had obtained our new Toyota, a white limousine, from the government almost free in spring 1988. Public officials only drove the car. It came with special equipment: an interior refrigerator, a dual-zone climate control, reading lamps, and automatic headlights. The interior was still wrapped in plastic when Salim parked our new car on our driveway.

Since Salim usually chauffeured my father in an SUV, my mother more often drove our new car.

---

8 born Audrey Kathleen Ruston (05/04/1929 - 01/20/1993), British actress, model, dancer, and humanitarian, recognized as a film and fashion icon

When my mother received her driver's license in 1973, she was one of the first women in patriarchal Mosul to drive a car. After Saddam Hussein seized power in 1979, women were given more freedom in many areas of life, such as getting (higher) education, work, and public childcare. He also established the Women's Union, which protected women's rights. Hence, it was normal by 1988 that women drove cars, moved freely, and to a greater extent wore modern clothes without covering their hair and body shape. Iraq had become more modern by 1988.

In the morning of August 6, 1988, *Rasala,* our housemaid, took the picture of my mother, who left our house.

Rasala looked after us with great care. For lunch, she sometimes even caught sparrows in our garden with bare hands to roast for us. I always watched her with large eyes, amazed and appalled by how quick and strong her hands were. She was my mother's age and also a Christian. During lunch, she always sat patiently next to us and waited until we ate up.

That day, my father came home from work early, in the afternoon. He took two weeks off since he wanted to spend the time with us during the school holidays. While we had often gone hiking in the mountains of Northern Iraq, he now planned a trip to Baghdad to show us, among other things, Lake Habbaniyah, a huge lake near the Euphrates River.

Before we left for our journey, he let me sit on the driver's seat of our Toyota, while he sat down on the passenger seat. At an age of almost 2 years, I could not see through the windshield, but I could reach the steering wheel. Excited, I honked the horn a dozen times. "Fasten your seat belt!" I said. "Ay, Sir! And you watch the street," he said, beaming, as if we were on a true ride. Indeed, we were—building our bond as father and son.

We appreciated the time with my father since we did not see him often. In addition to long working days in Mosul, his constant business trips led him to 43 countries by 1988. Each time he went abroad, he received an extra salary per day from the Ministry of Industry. His business trips usually took between ten and 15 days. When he returned, the salary he had earned usually equaled five months work in Mosul.

Lack of money had never been a problem for us.

Mid-August 1988

While flying was too expensive for most Iraqis and Germans, we flew to Germany every year to visit my grandmother in Amtal, a small village in Lower Saxony.

In August 1988, my mother was in her fifth month of pregnancy. *Hikmat,* our family doctor and friend, recommended that she go to Germany, where the climate was moderate, and give birth there. He was worried the heat in Iraq could lead to complications with her varicose veins and that the local doctors would not be well enough equipped to treat her even though the Iraqi medical facilities ranked as some of the best in the Arabic-speaking countries by 1988.

Monday, December 7, 1988

Sophia, my youngest sister, was born in December in the hospital of Oslar, a town near Amtal. My mother, Sophia, Nour, and I stayed in Amtal afterward, while my father and my other siblings had already flown back in September because of work or school.

Despite our five-month stay, I was too young to keep much of our visit in Germany in my mind.

Beginning of April 1989

Back in Mosul, my father surprised my brothers and me one day. He came home from work early, after Mamun and Alim had finished their afternoon school. "Follow me! I've got a surprise for you," he told us. He led us to the backyard, where we spotted three sheep grazing. "They are yours!" he said. We looked at him with big eyes and then at the sheep again. One sheep was white, the other had black ears, and the third was speckled black. Its mixed color captivated me. "Can I have the black and white one?" I asked, amazed. When they said, "Yes," I ran to hug it. Mamun and Alim followed and touched their sheep as well, yet more carefully since they were wearing fine fabric suits from my father's production. I, in contrast, was wearing a Mickey Mouse T-shirt and blue jeans, which I had already bedraggled with mud in the morning when I crawled around the bushes to collect snakes or scorpions in jam jars. "What a great present! Thank you Baba," I raved.

Compared to my siblings, I was keen to embark on adventures and test my boundaries. I stroked the sheep, climbed it, and learned that I could ride a sheep if I treated it gently.

End of August 1989

The table in our kitchen was not laid for breakfast when Mamun, Alim, and I went downstairs in the morning. Instead, my father was standing next to it. "We'll go to the hospital today. They'll cut off a small piece of your penis that you don't need," he told us.

"What? Cut off?" I said, terrified. Barely 3 years old, I tried to escape into the garden, but my father was faster than I was. He grabbed my arm while I was trying to run away.

"You have to do it. Otherwise, you don't become a real man," he said.

"I'm too small to become a man now. Leave me alone! I won't come," I retorted.

"I got circumcised, your brothers will be, everyone is. It's part of our religion."

"I don't want it!" I screamed.

"But you have to!" he shouted, pulling me outside while Mamun and Alim followed.

I was scared to death for the first time and quite rightly. During the surgery, I, in contrast to Mamun and Alim, who stood the operation well, died three times on the operating table after numerous respiratory and cardiac arrests. My small body did not tolerate the anesthesia. The doctors needed more than two hours to stabilize me.

Habitually, boys were circumcised between the age of 7 and 10, when religious rules were more and more introduced through family, institutions like schools and mosques, and the larger society. The circumcision of boys was not required in the Quran but in the Sunnah[9]. My father thought it would be a good opportunity to not only practice a religious tradition but also celebrate with family and friends his three male descendants all at once.

Friday, September 1, 1989

I was traumatized at the age of 3. In my dreams, I still saw myself lying on a white operating table, dead still, while doctors jumped around me. During the day, I could still smell the hospital's sharp disinfectant even though Rasala no longer used it to spare me.

On September 1, 1988, I also became aware of the metallic smell of blood. Our three sheep were slaughtered for the celebration of our circumcision. I was seesawing in the morning when my father and two other men took our three sheep behind a bush. Shortly after, I heard a hysteric bleat and then saw a stream of blood running onto the lawn. I shouted after my mother as loud as I could. When she came running, she

---

[9] traditional Muslim law based on the Prophet Muhammad's words and deeds

spotted the blood as well. She grabbed me and carried me to the kitchen. "Everything is fine," she said, trying to calm me down, while I could only cry. The sheep had been bought for that day in the first place, but nobody had told us. I felt sorry for the sheep and deceived by my parents.

In the afternoon, about 50 adults and a dozen children visited my family in our Mansur mansion to help us celebrate. We awaited them in the backyard, where some service people were putting the meat on the grill behind us. I still felt anguish about the loss of our sheep. Like Mamun and Alim, I had been dressed by my mother in a traditional costume. We three wore a white dishdasha[10] and a gold necklace with a Quran pendant, like my father. Everyone congratulated and kissed us on our cheeks more than the usual three times. Ammu[11] Nuri took pictures of us standing together on the lawn. My head almost reached my father's waist. He beamed intensely into the camera. My brothers and I smiled politely. After the photo shooting, our guests clapped their hands, while my penis was still hurting. I was overwhelmed by the bizarre dictate of culture. *I was no adult yet,* I sensed, *but only a 3-year-old, mutilated child that was in pain.*

While I questioned the ritual, I was also aware that my parents expected high standards of our behavior, especially in public. *Belonging to high society demanded being perfectly respectable, regardless of whether we liked it or not.*

---

10 ankle-length garment with long sleeves

11 Arabic, means "uncle" or used as a name for an elder out of respect

After my circumcision, I wore a dishdasha every day. I used to pull the piece of cloth aside, so that it would not rub on the wound. My father constantly warned me not to do it, especially in front of other people. Before our guests had come that day, he urged me again, "This is bad manners. Don't pull it! Don't say it hurts! You're a man." He also addressed Mamun and Alim with a serious face, "Don't put your elbows on the table! Don't eat much! Eat only when older people offer you something! And always listen to older people! Don't talk much! Talk only when older people ask you something!" They nodded silently. They had heard this type of directions many times before.

Even though I sensed the seriousness of that day, my need to protect myself prevailed. I pulled the dishdasha aside as often as I needed, especially after sunset when most adults moved inside to drink chai, while the children, including me, stayed outside to play hide and seek.

I was sitting behind a bush, waiting to be found when night drew in. It was unusual for me to stay outside at that late hour. Animals rushed by while bushes and trees rustled. The moonlight and uncountable stars illuminated the dark sky above me. Amazed, I listened to the beautiful whistles, thrills, and gurgles of a bird I had never heard before, accompanied by the chirping of crickets. I knew that the other children would need a while to find me. Leaves covered almost my entire body. *What an exciting night after all!*

Fall 1990

One morning, Salim drove my parents and me to some jewelry shops downtown to buy a necklace for Manal's wedding. Manal had met a man, *Amir,* at Mosul University a few weeks earlier and quickly got engaged with him. She was in love with his honey-colored eyes. Amir studied chemistry. He came from a poor background. His parents were Bedouins[12] and had 13 children, including Amir. Manal studied biology. According to custom, the groom gave jewelry equivalent to ten monthly salaries to his bride on the wedding, while parents bought practical things for the new household, such as furniture. My parents could afford to buy both.

Thursday, November 29, 1990

About 50 guests gathered in our Mansur mansion to celebrate Manal's wedding. Everyone was dressed formally. Manal and Ammu Amir were sitting on red armchairs at the end of our living hall. She was wearing a white dress. The golden necklace with the Quran pendant, which we had bought, was twinkling on her neck. Ammu Amir was wearing a fine anthracite suit. Behind them, hanging on the wall above our fireplace, the picture of my father and Saddam Hussein overlooked the scenery. I was sitting on a couch next to Mamun and Alim, who were

---

[12] a grouping of Arab ethnic groups, nomadic peoples of the Middle Eastern deserts, especially of North Africa, the Arabian Peninsula, Egypt, Palestine, Iraq, Syria, and Jordan

wearing tailored suits. I, in contrast, was wearing a green pullover with a biker logo and "FREESTYLE" printed in white letters, chest-high, over a white shirt. My mother had dressed me. She knew I did not like to wear tight suits, and she knew about my, in contrast to my siblings, strong will to go my way and resist the not very useful dictates of cultural tradition.

Three dining tables were arranged behind each other in the middle of our living hall. On the middle table, a three-tiered butter cream cake was waiting to be cut. "Let's first take a picture of the family and the bridal couple before we eat," my father told us. As we went to the front, I looked at Ammu Amir. He looked like Saddam Hussein with his black mustache, his stern look, and his wiry hair combed back. I was worried about the fact that he would take away my dear sister. "Watch out! Don't you treat Manal badly!" I told him with a raised finger. "Careful!" my father rapidly grabbed my arm. "What did I tell you? Don't talk!" he said. I looked at my father with lowered eyebrows. I did not like to be silenced; yet I felt guilty about not being the good boy he wanted me to be. So, I kept silent.

MONDAY, DECEMBER 24, 1990

I soon learned that Manal's wedding did not mean that she would leave us for good. In fact, we celebrated the next upcoming holiday, Christmas, like every year before.

In the morning, my mother, Manal, and Nour decorated a tall larch tree in our living hall with red ornaments, glass globes, golden gongs, and white candles. Sophia and I observed every step with big, shiny eyes. *Christmas was exceptionally colorful and beautiful.*

Even though they did not explain Christmas to Sophia and me, I noticed that it was under an extraordinary spell. It was different from the Muslim holidays we celebrated and yet similar in some ways. On the one hand, we were the only family I knew who celebrated Christmas and who, on top, would be visited by the bishop of Mosul on Christmas. On the other hand, our relatives and dozens of children from our neighborhood came to celebrate with us as if Christmas were a Muslim holiday. Of course, the small children marveled at our special tree, as Sophia and I did.

Ammu Nuri visited us at night. In contrast to the Muslim holidays, he was not wearing a dishdasha but his best suit when he congratulated my mother. Everyone was smiling. Underneath our tree, a sea of presents was spread out for all of us. Our record player filled the hall with Christmas music, which I enjoyed but did not understand since the lyrics were in German. *Still, Christmas was great—a time of togetherness, kindness, and joy.*

Thursday, January 10, 1991

Six weeks after Manal's wedding, Nour got married as well. She had met *Serhat* for the first time in fall 1990 when she had visited Manal at Mosul University. Serhat studied physics. He was a proud Kurd[13]. With his full and long brown hair,

---

[13] ethnic group in the Middle East, mostly inhabiting a contiguous area spanning adjacent parts of southeastern Turkey, northwestern Iran, northern Iraq, and northern Syria

he reminded Nour of *George Michael*[14], her favorite singer. Even though Nour was only 17 years old, and even though she did not graduate from high school yet, the wedding followed quickly. My parents barely had any time to comment on it.

We hosted about 150 guests. Our Mansur mansion was action-packed with chatting, laughing, and singing adults and children. Since my parents were busy attending to all our guests, I had more freedom to do what I liked. I was going from person to person, listening, laughing, talking, and running. *Another exciting night!*

I enjoyed my early childhood. Despite my parents' strictness, I felt loved and free most of the time. I felt connected to my family and to our friends, as well as to my thoughts, my emotions, and myself.

---

14 born Georgios Kyriacos Panayiotou (06/25/1963 - 12/25/2016), English singer, song-writer, record producer, and philanthropist, best known for his work in the 1980s and 1990s

II. In the Air And on the Road

◈

January-October 1991

"Fear and love need no language"

Thursday, January 17, 1991, 3 a.m.

I was sleeping soundly, wrapped in a warm, soft blanket. A blue flower pattern decorated my cover and my pillow. My mother had embroidered all our bedclothes.

Suddenly, the siren behind our backyard started howling. I woke up and looked outside the window with small eyes. Everything was dark, a total blackout. I was alarmed.

I got up to walk to my parents, but my mother was quicker. She tore open the door with Sophia on her arm. "Go downstairs, now!" she shouted. Something was seriously wrong, I sensed. I dashed after her to the hallway, where everyone was gathering. The whole family was there, apart from Nour, who stayed with Ammu Serhat in Duhok. While the siren wailed again, we rushed down to the first floor.

"Yallah![15]" my father shouted at us. I was frightened. *What was going on?* Downstairs, *Abu Rabi,* our personal bodyguard who lived across the street and who worked for the secret service, hastily opened our front door. "I'm obliged to tell you that you need to get out, now!" he shouted. "Every big city is a death trap now. You'll be brought to a safer place."

My father hugged us in a hurry, "Get in the car! Do exactly what you are told!"

We ran to our new white Mitsubishi Pajero. Salim already waited behind the steering wheel. Only after we had fastened our seatbelts did I notice that my father did not come.

---

15 Arabic phrase, means "hurry up"

"Wait! What about Baba?" I asked, grabbing my mother's shoulder from the rear seat.

But she remained silent.

"I'll bring you to a village, away from the targets. I know the people out there," Salim said. "Your father needs to stay close to the factory."

My mother looked at my father with tears in her eyes.

I banged my hands on the window. "Baba, come with us! Come with us!" I shouted while he stayed behind at the front door, looking at us, like a statue, with a terrified face.

"Abu Rabi will take care of him," Salim said.

That moment, Sophia also started crying, "Baba! Baba!"

Our protest was in vain, though. Salim switched on the engine. Before he found his way out, he bumped three times into our metal gate. He did not turn on the front lights, so that no one could spot us on our flight.

The U.S. led "Operation Desert Storm" began to target Mosul, the ancient metropolis, with tons of deadly weapons. We had just entered the road when I heard a howling sound rapidly coming from high in the sky down to earth. Shortly thereafter, an explosion occurred behind our backyard. It was the loudest, most terrifying bang I had ever heard, as if a massive part of the ground was abruptly breaking off miles deep into the earth's fiery core. Our car was shaking violently. My bones rattled. I felt a piercing pain in my chest. Once again, I was scared to death.

Abu Rabi drove down the main street at maximum speed. He drove through the barrier at the gate, crossed a ditch, the freeway, and another ditch before he hit bumpy desert soil. "The village is 30 miles west of Mosul," he said, while we remained tongue-tied.

As we stole away into the desert, Manal tried to cover my eyes since I could not stop looking outside the window. Warplanes continuously approached Mosul like gigantic buzz saws from above. Even though I could not detect them, their attacks were unmistakable. Every time they got closer, an aerial shrieking turned into an ear-splitting thunder while wailing lights incessantly rose from the ground into the sky, trying to stop the warplanes, but usually in vain. Intense lights, one after another, illuminated the ground. Every time a bomb was dropped, an abyssal bang and a shock wave haunted us. I felt the vibrations at the car door. The more bombs were dropped, the less I could see of Mosul. *Mosul was sinking in fire and dust.* I clung to Manal, speechless with terror.

We drove almost two critical hours in the desert under lethal warplanes since Abu Rabi repeatedly lost his way in the dark. After we had crossed a short bridge, we finally arrived at a walled-in village—Sheikh Ibrahim. Several men were standing in front of the village gate. They were covering their mouths with rags. I wondered why but remained speechless, weighed down by all the destruction I had seen. My body was shaking from fear.

Abu Rabi got out of the car and talked to an old man who wore a full beard and a dishdasha. After a minute, Abu Rabi came back and opened our doors. "You can get out now. My uncle will take care of you. I'll go back to Mosul now.

Inshallah[16], I'll come back in the next days with some supplies and, inshallah, your husband and Baba," he said.

I could hardly follow the events. While we got out of the car, another unit of buzz saws approached Mosul. I looked up to the red, cloudy sky, which was illuminated by the fires of Mosul. Three planes flew over us in a terrible roar, one after the other in rapid succession. The ground was shaking. Manal grabbed me under my arms and quickly followed the old man indoors.

"My house is my farm," the old man told us in a chesty voice. Sheep, donkeys, and chickens were running around us in panic on the dirt. "If you need the backhouse, find your way amidst the animals," he said, pointing to the left while guiding us through the animals.

We stopped in front of a small wooden barn door. "There are blankets in the closet," he said. My mother bent down and entered the chamber. We followed one after the other. A brown carpet covered the cold floor. Two mattresses were lying in the corner. The small chamber had no window. "Push the lock bar, so that you don't freeze. It might freeze tonight," he said. Next to the mattresses, we spotted a small, tubular metal stove. "Let me bring you some paraffin," he said and left.

We looked at each other, aghast and in disbelief. The entire situation seemed unreal. *Would we really stay in that farm?*

---

16   Arabic expression, means "God willing" or "if God wills"

After a few minutes, he, accompanied by his wife, came back with a bottle of paraffin. "The Sultans, ahlan wa sahlan! Please sit down," she said. As we all sat down, a smile appeared on her round face, framed by the white scarf she was wearing. "I've heard good things about you." She looked at each of us, "Masha'Allah! Lovely children."

"One is missing. We don't know where she is now. Maybe she's with her husband somewhere in Kurdistan," my mother said.

"I'm sure her husband takes care of her. I'll pray for them," she said, looking into my mother's glazed, blue eyes before she asked, "Tell me, how bad is it?"

That moment, my mother started whimpering.

I was almost paralyzed from shock. I felt sorry for my mother, and yet I was unable to help her. *Fortunately,* the old woman hugged her immediately. I had thought my mother would always be strong. Within two hours, nearly everything I had known that was safe was gone. I slowly pulled my knees up tight against my chest and remained quiet for the rest of the night while Mosul, *the place where my father stayed,* sank beneath tons of fatal bombs.

At dawn, I followed Mamun and Alim to the backhouse. We slowly crossed the inner courtyard. My feet were cold. My legs felt heavy as we walked amidst the animals. Hay, feces, and a smell of sheep lay in the air. "Wash your face, especially the salty traces from last night," my mother called behind me. She did not know that there was only a hole in a wooden, piddled board in the backhouse. I urinated and quickly left the stinky room. Mamun and Alim needed more time.

Outside, I looked around and gradually awakened to our new reality. There were no sweet scented roses. There was no washbowl, no tub, no hot water, no power, no refrigerator, and no personnel. *Nothing of my former life existed in Sheikh Ibrahim, except being with a part of my family. And yet, we were trapped with a few villagers in loam huts that did not differ very much from the sandy desert behind the yellow village wall.*

Half-desperate, half-curious about how we could live in Sheikh Ibrahim, I left the courtyard to explore the place. A strip of green grass had grown along a little stream in front of the village gate. It revitalized the desolate area. Comforted by the only fresh colors in sight, I smiled.

My mother observed me carefully from our chamber while I started to keep myself busy, picking up pebbles from the ground. She let me stay outside. She knew that sitting inside our chamber, inactive and facing raw uncertainty, would be too discouraging, too disturbing for me.

While I was collecting stones, a distant sound of an engine suddenly reached my ears. I turned around and detected a car on the horizon, driving toward Sheikh Ibrahim from Mosul, which had lost a number of tall buildings. *The car was white.* I ran to our barn door and shouted, "Everyone come! Abu Rabi is coming." My family came out immediately. We waited in front of the village wall, impatient and hopeful. "Your father is coming, too!" my mother noticed excitedly.

When Abu Rabi parked in front of us, my father jumped out of the car. We all hugged each other for a long moment. I felt safe again. *We are together again,* I thought. *Almost.*

"Any news from our daughter?" my mother asked.

"No," my father said, visibly worried. "How have you been?"

"We had no sleep. Mamun and Alim have diarrhea now. We need medicine," she said.

"I'll take care of that," he said. His legs began to shake, "They destroyed the factory."

She stared at him, bewildered and yet trying to keep her nerves. "Let me come with you. I will get the things we need here."

"I'll come, too!" I said, afraid I could lose both of them. However, they would not take any of us to Mosul since the next strike was possible at any time. Manal knew and held me back. I cried.

At around 4 p.m., Abu Rabi came back with my mother. I felt relieved to see her again and yet afraid for my father, who stayed in the city of death.

After all, some material things improved our stay. When Abu Rabi opened the trunk, I spotted plastic bags with salt, meat, and medicine, bottles with petroleum and water, and the embroidered blankets and pillows we had slept with the night before the war began.

End of January 1991

Despite Abu Rabi's regular supplies from Mosul, clean water remained scarce in Sheikh Ibrahim. It had to be collected from an olive grove that was 300 yards away. We had barely enough drinking water. My mother thus used our water sparingly. Only at night, when we gathered in our chamber, would she put a bowl on the stove to wash our faces and hands with warm water before we would lie down.

Sleep, however, was also scarce. After the first week, the bombardments decreased for a few days but then increased again. The heaviest strikes took place at 2 a.m. and 4 a.m. Every night I would lie close to my siblings and listen to the heavy warplanes that raged around us and dropped bombs everywhere. The unending echoes of explosions pierced the nightly air. Sometimes, when the bombs were dropped at the neighboring villages, I felt the vibrations in the ground. I was scared to death every night, *Would they also throw bombs on our heads?*

Usually, it took me more than one hour after the last strike to surrender to my fatigue and fall asleep for a few hours. There was one routine that calmed me down little by little: the soothing conversations of my mother. Despite the coldness, our barn door always remained a slit open since she could not fall asleep either. She would sit on the doorsill with *Umm Shihab,* the old woman, who came after the last strike with chai and kletsha[17]. Umm Shihab would tell stories about the city-people she had met. The even rhythm of her husky voice seemed to make my mother forget about the war and the cold. Sometimes, they even laughed together, which made me forget about our almost unbearable state for a moment.

---

17   yeast cookies filled with nuts or dates

Still, staying in Sheikh Ibrahim during winter increasingly drained our strengths. After breakfast, which consisted only of tea and flatbread with sesame paste or dates, my siblings and I usually left our chamber to play with the children of the five families from Mosul who also temporarily stayed in Sheikh Ibrahim. Even though the mornings were often so cold that we could see our breath, we kept the habit of playing outside. It was a good distraction. We usually played between the donkeys, geese, and chickens at the stream. Sometimes, we drew pictures in the mud with sticks. Even though my skin had cracked at many places because of the dry cold, even though dirt had gotten into my wounds, and even though the green pus blisters between my fingers hurt terribly, I absolutely wanted to play with the others. Yet, we never talked much. Only the animals around us made a sound every now and then. We could not escape reality. The longer we stayed in Sheikh Ibrahim, the weaker we got, physically and mentally, knowing that Mosul was being destroyed more and more. Our hope that we could live our old life again seemed to decrease every day.

One day, it rained nonstop. We stayed in our chamber. For the first time, I realized to a tiny degree that external power had a direct impact on my life. My mother and Manal asked themselves what would happen to us now that Saddam Hussein had put the world against Iraq by illegally invading Kuwait. I was deeply worried. The picture of my father and Saddam Hussein appeared before my eyes. *Would they punish my father now?*

"Is Baba bad? Like Saddam?" I asked my mother.

"No, he's good. And don't mention the other name! People are not supposed to speak about him," she said, agitated.

Saddam Hussein's regime proved to be brutally efficient. Whoever spoke against him had to be afraid of facing fatal consequences. Abduction, torture, and political murders were a daily occurrence. Paranoia among people was the result. I did not know about it at the age of 4.

Beginning of February 1991

Staying somehow active helped us escape the growing, dooming insecurities about our future and the fear of terror and death. Yet, it only helped a little and only for short moments before the insecurities and fears would re-emerge and dominate our existence.

One afternoon, my mother, Sophia, and I accompanied Umm Shihab to the olive grove. We wanted to collect some water. My mother carried Sophia on her arm. I toddled behind them on a stiff sand-trail until we reached a loam wall. Umm Shihab opened a wooden gate. When we entered the olive grove, my mother's face was suddenly shining all over. She smiled and marveled at the olive leaves shining silver-green.

"In Mansur, I watered every plant, even when the gardener hid from the heat. I also looked after our chickens," she said, suddenly wistful again.

Umm Shihab put her hands on her shoulders. "They'll still be there when you go back. Don't worry," she said consolingly and collected two buckets of water from the well.

On our way back, Umm Shihab walked far in front of us. I was walking behind my mother, who had Sophia on her arm, when I heard a sound suddenly breaking the sky behind us. I quickly looked over my shoulder. For the first time, I spotted the gigantic buzz saw at day light—*a gray warplane, like a huge bird.* My mother had watched out for it every time I played at the stream. *Now, our time was up.*

"Mama, wait! Carry me! So that they don't see me!" I shouted in panic, magically thinking, like a 4-year-old, that my mother could protect me from everything. She turned around and saw it coming, too. Terrified, she ran to me, grabbed me, and began to run with Sophia and me on her arms as fast as her legs could carry her.

We were 150 yards away from the village when the warplane began to hunt us with constant machine gun fire. The bullets exploded on the ground close to my mother's heels. Sand blasted into the sky. It almost threw her off balance, but she kept running and running. I held my breath. My heart cramped. Once again, I was scared to death.

Umm Shihab held the village gate open, screaming hysterically, "Allahu Akbar![18]"

---

[18] Islamic Arabic expression, usually translated as "God is [the] greatest," used in various contexts by Muslims, in formal prayer, in the call for prayer, as an informal expression of faith, in times of distress, or to express resolute determination or defiance

When we finally reached the gate, the warplane veered toward Mosul. It did not come back. The pilot spared us strangers. We had escaped death by a heel.

Mid-February 1991

After the incident with the warplane, which was an F-16 as my mother told me later, I was only allowed to go to the stream and no further. I understood the precaution. *The next plane could come anytime.* Hence, I examined the sky even more carefully whenever I left our chamber.

Sheikh Ibrahim sharpened my senses. Even though I did not know how long we had already stayed, I developed a feeling of the time of the day. I had begun to observe the calling for the prayer and the location of the sun. It gave me something to hold on.

One day, I was sitting at the stream when the sun was high in the sky. The adhan[19] for the noon prayer filled the air. Shortly after, I heard a car approaching. *It was Abu Rabi and Baba.* I shouted for my family. They came immediately and waited with me, impatiently.

Our only form of communication during the war was from person to person. As soon as my father got out of the car, we tightly hugged him. I felt relieved to know that he was still alive.

---

19 Islamic call to worship, recited by the muezzin at prescribed times of the day

"Our petrol reserve is running short. The military has drawn in everything. We have only one more chance to find Nour," he said to my mother.

She nodded. A tear rolled down her face.

I sensed that the situation was critical.

"You stay. We'll come back later," he told us.

I fell silent in grave fear. *What would happen if the petrol reserve did not suffice to find Nour, who needed our help? Would she die out there? Would I even lose my parents in the next strike?*

Fortunately, they came back in the afternoon, *even with good news.* They said they had found Ammu Serhat's cousin, who told them that Serhat and Nour found refuge in the mountains of Kurdistan with some other people. I felt temporarily relieved. We had been in the mountains during our short vacation trips. Pictures ran through my mind. We were playing hide and seek in small caves. *Nour could hide there from the war planes,* I imagined.

However, fear quickly followed my hope. *Our family was still separated from each other by the chaos of the war that could delete us without difficulty.* We lacked nutrition and a bombproof shelter. The medicine we had brought was supposed to last six weeks. Yet, we had used it up within two weeks. Only minimal hope remained—hope for the end of terror.

Sunday, March 3, 1991

Abu Rabi arrived in Sheikh Ibrahim around noon with big news. "The ceasefire conditions are set up. Iraqi troops are out of Kuwait. The U.S. and the other troops will soon move out as well. I'll bring you back home today," he said. "Alhamdulillah![20]" Manal said and hugged each of us. "We go to Baba, right?" I asked my mother. She nodded with a thoughtful smile. We collected our things within a few minutes and hugged everyone in the village to say goodbye. I was glad we could finally go home *where everything was beautiful and enjoyable*—I still believed.

Yet, my naive anticipation soon turned into distress. Entering Mosul, I felt the rubble from the destroyed city crushing under our wheels. No one was able to speak. We stared outside the window in disbelief. An endless picture of total destruction opened up in front of us. Streets were torn open. Buildings and bridges lay in ruins. Power poles were lying on the streets. We zigzagged through a city that I hardly recognized.

Mosul was strangely desolate. The small cabin next to our gated community was not manned. The barrier, which had secured the gate, lay on the street, broken. We drove over it in a knocking sound. "Where are all the people?" Alim asked, but he did not receive an answer.

After a moment, Manal said, "Mosul is not only destroyed. It's dead." She broke out in tears while I was sitting on her lap, feeling sorry and helpless.

When we stopped at our house and got out of the car, we spotted blood spots curled on the sidewalk, leading to our neighbors' car. Their car was burnt out. Pictures of our flight

---

20 Arabic phrase, means "Praise be to God"

ran through my mind. *The death from above must have killed them.* I was horrified.

Suddenly, my father spoke to us from behind. We turned around. "Don't be shocked. Nothing is cleaned up. I told our personnel to go home," he said. We hugged him at the front door. I felt relieved—until he showed us around our house, so we could see what damage the war had caused. Some interior doors were lying on the floor, blasted out. The windows were blasted, too. Shards of glass covered the ground. Our Christmas tree was lying on the floor. The ornaments were broken, the curtains and couches tattered; the picture of my father and Saddam Hussein was lying on the floor under shards of glass. *The bombs destroyed our beautiful home.* I was shaken.

Heavy-hearted, I followed my family outside. We crossed the lawn and headed to the mesh wire enclosure. All the chickens were lying on the soil, dead.

"They must have had a heart attack," my mother said. Tears filled her eyes. "There were too many targets next to Mansur. The power plant. The military base. The airport," my father said with a gloomy face.

Mournful, we continued on our lawn that was partly covered with bricks. The backyard wall had several large holes. Some trees were uprooted. Shells were swimming in our pool. All the destruction was ungraspable to me until I grabbed some shells and looked at them. My father took a slow breath and said tiredly, "Leave them; they're not toys." I threw them back to the water. We looked at the factory behind our rosarium. The power and the storage building were in ruins.

"What will happen now?" my mother asked with quiet despair.

"I don't know," my father paused. "The currency is worthless now. The bombs were just the beginning. Now, the UN[21] sanctions will hit us even more," he said ominously.

I did not understand what he meant, but I understood that the beautiful and enjoyable times were over.

"What about Yarmouk?" she asked.

"We'll go and stay there at first. It's not as damaged like our house here."

"Can we go to school again?" Mamun asked.

"There's no school, habibi[22]. You just stay at home for the time being," he said.

Shattered, we walked back to our house to collect some things for Yarmouk.

END OF APRIL 1991

In Yarmouk, my father repeatedly told us that the UN sanctions regime in Iraq had banned the manufacture of chlorine and radically restricted its import. I did not understand what that meant, but I soon faced the consequences of contaminated

---

21 United Nations, intergovernmental organization to promote international co-operation

22 Arabic, means "my darling"

water that could not be treated with chlorine. Even though my mother always boiled the tap water before she gave it to us, I woke up with severe diarrhea one day. I was unable to hold any nutrition. After two days, I was too weak to move.

I was lying on the sofa in our living room when she washed my face and I fainted. Hikmat came within minutes. He gave me an injection. Slowly, I became conscious again.

"We've got 24 hours, probably less. He's too weak," Hikmat said.

My father spoke straight into his face, "Do something!"

"I've used up all my medicine. The local hospitals don't have any, either. I had hundreds of such cases in the last few weeks. It always first hits the young, under the age of five," he said.

My mother turned her back toward us. "Ya Allah![23] Not another son," she cried.

"I know a doctor in Samarra. He's a good friend of mine. It's 350 miles round-trip. Maybe he has got the shot. I'll drive there and check now," Hikmat said.

My father nodded—staring at him. "What can we do?"

"Take him to the hospital. They might take away his pain at least. I'll meet you there."

Late at night, Hikmat came with the shot I needed. I was lucky.

Children my age who were not from families held in high esteem and who did not have special connections died

---

23 Arabic, means "my dear God"

because of polluted water. Diarrhea, gastroenteritis, and cholera, which had almost been defeated before the sanctions, killed thousands of children within a few months while the mainstream world community was either not informed or did not care.

Thursday, May 16, 1991

During the day, my father often left the house to meet with public officials and inquire about Iraq's future. Usually, he came back for dinner in the evening.

One evening, he made a crucial announcement while we, except for Manal and Nour, who were with their husbands, were eating potato casserole at the oak corner booth in our kitchen.

"Tomorrow, we go to Amman. We will stay there till things improve here," he said.

My mother looked at him with big eyes, "What about school? It starts soon."

"Nothing will be like it used to be. They won't order new books. There'll be shortages of food, medicine, services, and much more. We need to get out now while it's still possible."

"And leave everything behind?" she asked.

He looked at her with a rigid face and nodded.

She put down her fork, visibly weighed down by concerns, and nodded slowly. It seemed as if escape was our only option.

I felt troubled. *My parents,* my guardians, *were forced to take us from our beloved home.*

After dinner, we packed 13 suitcases. It was not the first time we would travel to Amman, Jordan. We had vacationed there before. Yet, it was the first time we did not know whether we would come back home. I felt anxious because of the uncertainty of our future.

Friday, May 17, 1991

Apart from Manal and Nour, who stayed with their husbands, we escaped from Mosul with an old taxi at night.

I was sleeping until sunrise when my father announced from the passenger seat, "We're close to the Jordanian border. I've been told it's almost impossible to cross, but they might make an exception for us. Just let me talk. If anyone asks you, we're vacationing in Amman. Period!" Everyone nodded. *The situation was dead serious.*

Our driver stopped 20 yards in front of the border, which was patrolled by a dozen soldiers. Some were pointing their machine guns at us. My heart began to race. *Would they shoot us?*

Two soldiers approached us. While one asked our driver to lower the window, the other kept pointing his machine gun at us. At the soldier's request, my father handed out our documents. The soldier looked at them with narrow lips before he called for reinforcements.

Next, he asked us to get out of the car. Two additional officers opened the trunk. They rummaged our suitcases while the other two soldiers started a discussion with my father. The procedure took one hour, but my father stayed peaceful the entire time. *Somehow, he convinced them with his persistent calmness to open the border.* Once again, he proved to be my hero. I was thankful we stayed alive, thankful that they let us pass, and yet I wondered, *What was waiting for us in Amman?*

In Amman, our driver dropped us off at a tall, white building with five stars: the Amman Marriott Hotel. As we walked in the foyer, *Oventin,* my father's Taiwanese business partner and friend, and a dozen other people I did not know walked up to us. Most of them hugged and kissed us. One man introduced himself with a handshake as the cousin of a Jordanian Minister.

"I checked you in already. I didn't believe I'd ever see you again. I managed to get out before everything began," Oventin said to my father. "Let's celebrate! The Sultan family is alive. You're my guests the entire time you're in Amman, anything you want!"

His big smile made us smile as well.

"I'm so glad to see you, my friend! But let me pay. We're on our vacation. How did you know we were coming here?" my father said.

"Are you kidding? I thought the next time I would see you would be at your funeral. No way! Your family is my guest!" he paused. "I was looking for you and asked around!"

An excited, middle-aged couple came up to my siblings and me, "We reserved a room in the restaurant. You must be hungry and thirsty. We'll wait for you there." I felt welcomed and appreciated.

My parents thanked everyone and excused us. We took the elevator to our suite. A bouquet of roses and a basket with fruits awaited us on a table. I bent down to smell the sweet fragrance. The roses smelled as good as in Mosul. I smiled again.

After we had freshened ourselves up, we went downstairs to the restaurant. Oventin had already ordered plenty of food. We sat down at a long table. As we started to eat, the adults began to talk about old times. Time and again, they laughed out loud. I was full after two plates and got up with Mamun and Alim to collect the empty Pepsi cans. We piled them up on the red carpet. One tower held my height, nine cans. While my mother was taking some pictures, my father and the Taiwanese ambassador, who had also dined with us, were interviewed for what would become the headline of a newspaper article, "Taiwan Rescues the Sultan Family." Oventin would feel pleased about the successful escape story.

Tuesday, June 25, 1991

We stayed in Amman for six weeks. Almost every night, we were invited by Oventin or other business partners and friends to celebrate in exclusive restaurants. Grilled meat, tabbouleh[24],

---

24 Arabic, Levantine vegetarian dish, bulgur with parsley, tomatoes, and lemon

lentil soup, fruits, and much more was served on porcelain dishes on extended tables while waitresses poured drinks under shining chandeliers.

One evening, the German Consulate General dined with us as well. She told my father she would try to get us six-month visas to Germany—the beginning of a plan that would take shape.

A few days later, on June 25, my father called us in our suite to make another announcement that would change our life forever. He asked us to sit at the round table in the living room. "Today, our vacation ends. Your flights are in the afternoon," he said in a serious voice.

"Do we go home?" I asked, expectant.

"No. You'll go stay with your grandmother in Amtal, Germany," he told us.

My mother asked with big eyes, "What about our daughters?"

"They're married now. Their husbands will take care of them; and I will, too," he said.

"And you? Why don't you come with us?" Mamun asked.

"Because it's complicated for me to leave. But you can go to Germany, where it's save," he said.

I was scared for my father and yet too young to understand the pressure he faced in Iraq and how difficult it was for a prominent person like him to get a visa and leave the country.

My mother probably did. Still, she stared at him, shaking her head. "I can't manage that. My nerves are already raw because of the war. I can't start from zero with four small children with a husband somewhere abroad. I am 47 years old. What are you thinking?"

"If we go back to Iraq, the boys will be drafted soon, if they don't die beforehand from an illness. Our children can't live in Iraq, you know that." He raised his voice, "Iraq is done for the next 25, if not 50 years. Even the public officials admit that!"

Once again, I felt troubled. *My parents were forced to remove us from our home even further.* On top, I strangely felt unprotected. "What shall I do in Amtal alone?" I asked him.

"You'll not be alone. Your brothers, your mother, and Sophia will be with you," he said.

Yet, I did not believe him, assuming that Mamun and Alim would be at school all day and afterward plan their together-activities, while my mother would be out like so often when we still lived in Mosul. Besides, Sophia was only 2 years old, a quiet toddler that often slept half of the day.

My parents got up without another word and went to their bedroom to back our bags.

I followed them. "Baba, I'll come with you," I said with tears in my eyes.

"No, habibi. Go back to the living room and let us pack your things," he said.

He let out the air of my red swimming tube that was lying on their bed. The corners of my mouth turned down. Tears began to roll, but he did not dare to look at me. "Please, go, habibi," he said

I went to the living room, threw myself on the couch, and cried my eyes out. Even though I was too young to articulate the complex break in my family, I sensed that it was severe.

After two hours, a taxi drove us to Queen Alia International Airport. Our friends followed us in another taxi. They checked in our baggage and walked us to the gate.

"Be careful. Ba'ath[25] Party members can get into trouble now," Oventin told my father.

"Baba, don't go back to Iraq! They'll kill you there," I said, afraid of Saddam Hussein.

"Don't speak like that! Abu Rabi takes care of me. Don't worry," he said.

My mother looked at him with big tears in her eyes.

He sighed, "It's still possible to exit now. The minister recommended it and our mayor as well. I dearly hope that we, inshallah, will live together soon."

He turned to Alim and Mamun, "You're smart boys; you just finished primary school with excellent grades. You'll manage in Germany. And always listen to your mother!"

"Yes Baba," they chorused.

Next, he turned to me, "I know you're strong. But always listen to your mother!"

"Yes, and you come to Germany soon!" I said.

---

25 Arabic, means "renaissance" or "resurrection," political party that mixed ideology of Arab nationalism, pan-Arabism, Arab socialism, and anti-imperialism, dissolved in 2003

He hugged each of us while I, grief-stricken and shaking from fear, was feeling as if I saw and touched my father for the last time. The separation was unbearable for me. I was 4 years old.

At noon, we took off with Royal Jordanian Airlines. My father, my elder sisters, our beloved, caring relatives, our faithful employees, our good friends, our ample, sweet-scented gardens, our wild animals, the far-reaching metropolis, the majestic Tigris River, and all the people who respected and appreciated us, Mosul, the place I thought of as my home, where I felt loved, where I could just be—everything was left behind. Mosul became a painfully pinched-off place in my heart, even if I was not fully aware of it yet.

We landed in Frankfurt in the afternoon. Not knowing what we would be facing in Germany and worried about the unknown, I followed my family inside the airport building. Hordes of people were cutting in and out, rushing from all directions to baggage claim. Some people talked in Arabic, but most spoke unfamiliar languages. I stopped walking and looked around with big eyes. I was overwhelmed with new impressions. Mamun looked over his shoulder for me. "Yallah, follow us!" he said. *Abu Rabi and Salim were missing, too,* I noticed. Feeling strange, small, and vulnerable, I caught up.

My mother and Mamun each got a baggage cart. After we had loaded the carts, we rushed to customs. Officers in green uniforms ransacked our luggage. My mother had neatly packed our clothes. After the search, our suitcases did not close anymore. With a wrinkled forehead, she swiftly folded our clothes together and put them into our suitcases. Some passengers behind us groaned impatiently. "Hurry up mummy," a man in a suit said, annoyed. I wanted to help her, but I was too little to reach the desk. I stayed close to her, hoping she would stand up to the pressure. *Fortunately, she did.*

"Follow me to the arrival hall!" she said. We walked on gray granite flooring to a large hall. Countless people were standing around, some were sitting and chatting, some were sleeping. Suddenly, someone waved his hand. *"Onkel Walter!"* she said and smiled. *Onkel who?* I did not remember him from our previous visits since we usually stayed with my grandmother. Onkel Walter had short, brown hair. He was one head taller than my mother was. After he had hugged her and told her some words in German, which I did not understand, he gave each of us a firm handshake. I felt tensed up and nervous about the uncertainties that awaited us. *What would happen next?* I knew that this stay would be different from our previous, short ones.

We followed him to the underground garage, where we got into an old, sandy station wagon. While we left the airport area, I looked outside the rear window. The freeway was clean. Trees were full with green leaves. Fields were systematically arranged and cultivated. I was impressed. Germany, in contrast to war-torn Iraq, seemed in perfect order.

After a 15-minute drive, we exited the freeway at a sign that contained non-Arabic letters. Even though I could not read, I was aware of the different letters. "We're in Kastel," my mother announced. The name sounded unfamiliar to me. Shortly, we stopped next to a property that was veiled by green cypresses. The place looked unfamiliar to me as well. I felt tense again. *What would be waiting for us behind this wall of trees?*

We entered the property on a path that contained countless pebble stones. Compared to the smooth, pre-fabricated pathway in Mosul, it felt edgy, almost unsafe to walk on that path. To my right, I spotted a lush lawn. The grass blades were thinner and greener than in Iraq. Several unrecognizable trees had grown in this garden, which was smaller than our backyard in Yarmouk. Yet, its vivid greenness made me hold my breath. Behind the trees, I spotted a sailboat on a terrace, parked upside-down on red bricks. The same bricks comprised the house facade. The first floor had a pitched roof. I had never seen such a steep roof before, and it almost looked dangerous to me. As we walked around the house, a row of fir trees cast a dark shadow on us. Even though it was summer, the temperature was mild in contrast to Iraq, I noticed.

Arriving in Germany, I became a stranger to myself. New impressions, unknown thoughts, and mixed feelings occupied me while I could not hold them back. It suddenly felt as if I lost control of my life even though I had barely thought about controlling my life in Iraq.

Through a backdoor, we entered a small, smoky hallway. My mother turned to us and announced, "Your uncle flies to Mallorca with his family today. We can stay here for a while. Follow him to the living room. I'll call grandmother now." Shyly, we did as we were told. I sat down at a wooden dining table. Sometimes, I dared to look at Onkel Walter. He was smiling, but he avoided eye contact. *Did he enjoy having us in his home?* I wondered.

After a short while, my mother joined us. With tears in her eyes, she said, "Nour will fly to Frankfurt Thursday night." It took me a moment to understand what she had said. *Nour was alive! Moreover, she would be back in our life!* Mamun, Alim, Sophia, and I got up full of joy.

Friday, June 29, 1991

When the morning sun sneaked through the shutters, I woke up with *Nour* on my mind. Happy, I walked upstairs and carefully opened the loft room door. The room was heated up. Nour was lying on a king-sized bed. Slowly, she turned her face toward me. She had dark circles around her eyes. Her bones stuck out from her skinny face. I was shocked by her look.

"Habibi, Junis. Come to me. Don't be afraid," she whispered in a weak voice.

I slowly walked to her and sat down at the edge of her bed. She sat up. Her skeleton body was covered with white, shapeless clothes. *She looked like a ghost.*

"We survived," she whispered.

"How are you?" I dared to ask.

"I'm good now. Ammu Serhat and I fled by foot to Turkey," she paused. "Oventin found me in a refugee camp with the help of the Turkish embassy." She breathed in and out, deeply, as if she had to recover from the words she had said and collect some strength to continue speaking. "After Baba had initiated my visa application from Mosul, I was driven to Istanbul. I stayed in a Catholic church until I was allowed to fly to Germany," she said.

I sensed that her flight was at least as traumatizing as ours had been. With tears in our eyes, we hugged each other. I was thankful to know that she was safe and that we were together again.

Tuesday, July 23, 1991

Four weeks passed by quickly. While my mother repeatedly went to administrative offices during the days, Nour looked after us as far as possible. She was six months pregnant and weighed only 88 pounds when she had arrived in Kastel. We were glad to see that she soon regained some weight and strength. Sometimes, she felt strong enough to come downstairs and join us in the living room. Occasionally, we watched Sesame Street all together. When it was aired, I asked my siblings what it was about. Yet, they did not understand German either. Anyway, the program seemed appealing and fun to me. Even so, we rarely watched television since my mother did not want to boost Onkel Walter's electricity bill. Most of the time, we just stayed at home, rested, and waited for my mother to come back.

When Nour felt particularly well, she sometimes even took us to the playground close by and bought us chocolate at the kiosk. I appreciated these small gifts. Even though I had no idea how much money we had, I knew that it was not much anymore. My mother repeatedly told us that we now had to spend our money very carefully. She spoke Arabic with us. She did not start teaching us German. It was easier for everyone, she sensed, since we were all too engrossed in finding ourselves again after all the destruction and loss we had experienced. Except for the language we used, Arabic, we had largely become strangers to ourselves.

When Onkel Walter and his family returned from their vacation, we had to leave the same day. "The house does not have enough space for two families," he told my mother. I was perplexed. In Mosul, our relatives often slept over on mattresses in our houses, unannounced, even in our smaller house in Yarmouk. *In Kastel, things seemed to work differently.*

After we had packed and brought our suitcases to the living room, Onkel Walter confronted my mother again, "650 DM[26] telephone bill? What did you do when I was away?"

She turned red in the face. "Did you use the phone?" she asked us.

"Sometimes. I had to call my husband. He's stuck in the camp," Nour said.

---

26 Deutsche Mark, the official currency of Germany until the adoption of the Euro in 2002

My mother raised her voice, "This is our entire welfare income I have to pay back to your uncle now. How could you do that? Have you lost ..."

Onkel Walter interrupted with a loud and clear voice, "Stop it! I don't want any trouble in my house. Get to the car now! All of you."

Everyone turned quiet at once. I was worried. *Were we in serious trouble?*

After a moment, Alim broke the silence, "Where are we going now?"

"To your grandmother," my mother said in a low voice.

I felt desperate. *How long could we stay there? And what would happen thereafter?*

On our three-hour trip to the north, I often stared outside the window, pondering. I was almost 5 years old when I became aware that my previous life was lost. I had no father, no big sister, no clan, no friends, no helpers, no language that other people spoke, no idea about how things worked in a seemingly strange country, and no home where I was accepted and appreciated. Money, food, and medicine were scarce, too. My teeth were rotting due to malnutrition. High society life was what I missed least. I felt without shelter. All I wanted was to have the whole family united again, to feel accepted and appreciated again, to feel happy and at peace again.

After all, I was lucky again. *Oma Erika,* my grandmother, awaited us in Amtal, a rural village with a few hundred inhabitants. She was 75 years old. 2,500 miles and more than 30 years had separated us most of the time, but her love did not dwindle away. At around 4 p.m., we parked in front of her trelliswork fence. Shortly after, she opened the front door. She clung to the stair railing and did not hesitate to take the pain of walking down the stairs. Her hair, tinged in gray, was proudly pinned up. We got out of the car and met her. She gave each of us a warm hug and announced, "Ihr seid hier immer willkommen, egal was passiert. Hier seid ihr in Sicherheit."

I did not understand what she said. *But love needs no language,* I learned. She took me by the hand and led us inside the kitchen. With a contented smile, she opened the fridge that was filled with food, "Guckt, meine Lieben, wir haben Wurstsalat, Schillerlocken, frischen Käseaufschnitt, Butter und noch viel mehr. Und frisches Brot ist auch da." Next, she grabbed her walking stick and led us to the living room, a clean and spacious room with a shiny, oak parquet floor and antique furniture. Golden embroideries decorated a green corner sofa. Thick, red curtains were draped around the room. Delighted by the beautiful sight, I smiled.

When Onkel Walter entered the living room with two suitcases in his hands, my mother asked us to collect the rest from the car and bring it to the second floor, which we did. Upstairs, more pleasant surprises awaited us. *The rooms were cozy and colorful.* One bedroom was painted sun yellow, the other rose, and the last turquoise. There was a bed for each of us with pillowy blankets and cushions. New coloring books and pencils were waiting on the desks. The bathroom had toothbrushes, towels, and two washbowls. The kitchen had a fridge with more fresh food. The house was even slightly bigger than ours in Yarmouk, I noticed, impressed.

Joyfully, we walked back down to the kitchen. Oma Erika announced with a sense of responsibility, "Am Montag haben wir einen Doktortermin. Ihr werdet dann komplett untersucht. Aber jetzt feiern und essen wir erst einmal." I understood the word "doctor" and smiled, knowing that *Oma Erika was going to take great care of us*. With a happy face, she led us through a French door to her veranda. The table had already been set for lunch. We sat down. Oma Erika smiled and so did we. I felt warmly welcomed again.

Moving north had been cold in many ways, so I enjoyed the warm atmosphere at Oma Erika's. *Being with her felt like family.*

Thursday, August 15, 1991

Oma Erika used to be a teacher and thus taught us German on every occasion. When we did grocery shopping, when we set the table, when we prepared lunch, she taught us the essential German words and let us repeat them every day. We also collected bowls of food directly from the garden. Rotkohl (red cabbage), Karotten (carrots), Kopfsalat (lettuce), Lauch (leek), Rhabarbar (rhubarb), and Zwiebeln (onions), I learned with interest, grew in the patch in front of the veranda. She also taught us the names of the fruits that grew along the back trelliswork fence: Äpfel (apples), Birnen (pears), Himbeeren (raspberries), and Brombeeren (blackberries).

My siblings and I loved spending time with Oma Erika in Amtal. From the backyard, we could look out over a valley with green meadows, cows, and sheep. The meadow was surrounded by a beautiful dark green, mixed forest. *Amtal was joyful and peaceful—like the time with Oma Erika—*and it almost made me forget about Mosul.

In addition to teaching us German on everyday life occasions, Oma Erika had started practicing the German alphabet with Mamun and Alim to prepare them for school. Every day, they sat down at the small kitchen table, where she dictated letters to them and after a little while words and small sentences. I often watched them and listened carefully.

On August 15, Mamun and Alim had their first school day. We all got up at 5 a.m. when my mother woke them up. We were excited for them to finally go to school again. *They always attended school in Mosul with joy and pride.* The school bus left at the pond near to Oma Erika's house at 6 a.m.

We awaited them on our driveway in the afternoon. As they approached the trelliswork fence, Mamun suddenly started to wail. I had never seen him so desperate. I was appalled.

"Mamun, habibi, what happened?" my mother asked, rushing toward him. He could not answer, though. He lost himself in an uncontrollable sobbing. She hugged him for a long moment while Oma Erika walked to him with her cane. He said, too embarrassed to look anyone in the eyes, "The children peed in my water bottle and laughed at me throughout the day because I, unknowing, almost drank from it."

I felt so sorry for him for what he was experiencing. He always tried to be like our parents wanted us to be, but now he was not perfect anymore. He could not speak proper German fluently, and he looked different with his curly, brown hair and relatively brown skin. His recognizable difference was considered as inherently negative. As a result, he was bullied.

Oma Erika took him by the hand and walked with him to the kitchen, "I know the principal. I'll call him right now and make sure that such a thing will not happen again."

Before she dialed the number, she asked Alim about his day.

"I felt like an alien," Alim said.

I was alarmed. Alim had straight hair like me but a lighter skin, and even though he was more outgoing than any of us was, he struggled to find friends.

That moment, I developed a new fear. *If my big brothers weren't so big anymore, what would the other kids do to me?*

Friday, August 30, 1991

We made a few friends in Amtal. Some children, especially the elder, usually ignored us on the playground. Some of the younger were told by their parents to leave us alone; and some were allowed to play with us since their parents knew my grandmother well.

Oma Erika helped us make friends by also inviting other children and their parents over. We often played on the driveway with the toys she gave us. Mamun and Alim tried to speak German every now and then, while I avoided it. I was too afraid of making mistakes and being bullied. *Luckily, playing did not depend on the German language.*

SATURDAY, AUGUST 31, 1991

Despite my new fear of being inadequate and rejected, I knew I could count on Oma Erika. She was one of the most caring people I knew. *She was sensitive to our feelings and met our needs as best as she could.* She hugged and praised us every morning and spent a lot of time with us every day. She taught us how to do the housework efficiently. She paid for all our spare time activities without hesitating: outdoor clothes, books, and tickets. Sometimes, she even spoiled us. When the mobile shop rang its bell, she would go with us outside and not only buy fresh, expensive food, but also give each of us a 1 DM coin, so we could buy what we liked. Usually, I bought a Kinder Surprise (a chocolate egg with a toy inside). The chocolate tasted sweeter than in Iraq and melted so gently in the mouth.

On my fifth birthday, Oma Erika gave me 20 matchbox sized cars. I smiled all over my face when I opened the present in the veranda. My siblings and I sat down on the carpet. We began to excitedly fire the cars to each other. Nour watched us with a glowing, smiling face, wearing her maternity dress. I was full of joy. *What a happy birthday!*

In the afternoon, we all sat down at the corner bench in the veranda to celebrate with tea and cake. After everyone had sung Happy Birthday to me in German, English, and in Arabic, we tasted from my mother's butter cream cake and the pastries Oma Erika had bought: streuselkuchen, elephant ears, and vanilla pudding cake with a thick chocolate icing on top, which was my favorite.

When Oma Erika's elder neighbor came over to take a picture of us, our loss overwhelmed me yet again. *What a sweet but also bitter moment,* I sensed. Painful questions suddenly stormed my mind. *Why could my father and Manal not be with us? Were they even still alive? Why did all this happen to us? Could we ever go back to Mosul?* I broke out in tears. No one could calm me down while I felt a pressure to understand my strange behavior. Yet, I was unable to grasp the complex emotions that pulled me down.

Beginning of September 1991

The longer we stayed in Amtal, the more telephone calls we received from Turkey during the nights. Since we slept upstairs, we often did not hear the ringing. Usually, Oma Erika, who slept on the first floor, picked up the telephone. "Hier ist *Linde,*" she would say, while the person on the other line would respond in Arabic. She would walk to the hallway and shout, "Phone call from Turkey." So, the yelling would start all over again. "Why can't they call in the daytime for God's sake!" my mother would shout at Nour. Usually, Ammu Serhat was on the phone, asking if we could help him and his family get from the refugee camp to Germany. Nour would then beg my mother, but my mother would respond in an angry voice, "They can't come, period! It'll get too crowded. Oma Erika will kick us out." Nour would begin to cry while I would listen to everything from my bed. The longer we stayed in Amtal, the more the nightly yelling and crying robbed our sleep and shredded our nerves.

Gradually, my halfway resecured life was unsettled again, not by war, but by the fighting between those nearest to me.

The increasing suffering and inaccessibility of my mother affected me most. She knew she was putting a big burden on Oma Erika because of Nour's relatives, and yet she didn't know how to solve the problem. She became very irritable. Sometimes, she shouted at us for no reason. Sometimes, she cried. Soon, she hardly ate or drank and rapidly lost weight. Nour and Oma Erika stayed quiet but also tense, while I wandered around in an emotional minefield, trying to find a sense of security in my family, in vain.

Beginning of September 1991

The telephone rang in the evening. Onkel Walter informed my mother that he had signed a purchase agreement for a house in Kastel that he would rent to us. He earned well as a chemical doctor and department manager in a chemical concern in Frankfurt.

My mother informed us about the agreement right after their talk. I was happily surprised even though I would have liked to stay with Oma Erika. Yet, I also knew that my mother wanted to be a minimum burden on her. Oma Erika had lived alone for many years. She had a strictly organized daily routine: getting up at 5 a.m., washing her hair, preparing the kitchen, having breakfast at 7 a.m., lunch at 12 a.m., one hour rest at 1 p.m., coffee at 3 p.m., dinner at 7 p.m., going to bed at 9 p.m. *Including six refugees in her routines was not easy. Keeping her routines while even more refugees continuously pressed to come was impossible.*

Tuesday, September 17, 1991

Despite the difficulties in our family, we kept our routines of togetherness.

One evening, we were all sitting at the round table in the living room, watching the 8 p.m. news on ARD[27]. The news anchor announced, "In Hoyerswerda, Saxony, an 11-story residential home of guest workers was attacked by 30 to 40 neo-Nazis. Stones, bottles, and Molotov cocktails were thrown. The building was set on fire. Hundreds of German residents joined the mob and applauded. The police retreated. Shortly after, a house of asylum seekers was attacked. 32 people were beaten, cut, or burned."

I did not understand most words, but I understood the violent pictures. I was scared.

After a politician commented on the problem that a large number of asylum seekers had come from Eastern Europe, Africa, and the Middle East to Germany, Mamun asked my mother in Arabic about the meaning of asylum seekers.

She said, gazing at the television screen with an upset face, "People who flee to another country because of war or because they're treated badly in their home country."

"Like us?" I asked.

"No," she promptly said, "I'm German, and you will be soon, too."

---

27 Arbeitsgemeinschaft der öffentlich-rechtlichen Rundfunkanstalten der Bundesrepublik Deutschland, Consortium of public broadcasters in Germany

"Will they kill us?" I asked.

"No," she turned to me and shook her head. "You live with your grandmother and not in such a building, and your grandmother is German, too."

Still, I felt alarmed. *Was she only pretending to calm us down? Why then did they pee in Mamun's bottle? And why did some parents not allow their children to play with us?*

Friday, September 20, 1991

The bell rang in the morning. Oma Erika opened the front door, and there he stood, unannounced: Ammu Serhat. We met in the living room. I hardly recognized him. His bones stuck out of his face, and he was wearing a full beard. No one dared to say a word. Suddenly, the telephone rang. Nour picked it up. His relatives were calling. She looked at Oma Erika, "Please, help us." But Oma Erika raised her voice, "I can't take more. If it doesn't stop, you'll all have to leave!" Nour ran out of the house. Ammu Serhat followed her. My mother started to cry. She sat down at the desk and sent a teletext to my father, "If you don't come now, you'll visit me at my grave. Serhat and his relatives cause a lot of problems. If they don't leave us in peace, my mother will kick us out." Shortly after, she fainted on the desk. Oma Erika rushed to the phone and dialed the emergency number, but that moment my mother regained consciousness. I was watching everything, standing next to the sofa, helpless and aware, *My family urgently needed help.*

Mid-October 1991

Fortunately, my father managed to come. He called my mother right after he had landed in Frankfurt. We were sitting in the living room, listening with eager eyes to their talk. He told her that he would first get a car from a colleague, a small Volkswagen, and then come to Amtal. We looked at each other and smiled. I was looking so forward to finally seeing him again for the first time since Amman. I missed him more than words could say.

He arrived the next day in the afternoon. I hugged him on the driveway for a long moment, relieved to see him alive and overjoyed to be with him.

Tuesday, October 31, 1991

My siblings and I woke up around 4 a.m., alarmed. Nour was screaming in pain while she was walking down the stairs with Ammu Serhat. Oma Erika and my parents were waiting in the hallway on the first floor. When Nour arrived downstairs, two first aiders came in and carried her outside on a stretcher. Ammu Serhat followed them. *She was about to give birth!* I was excited for her to become a mother and for our family to grow but also worried about her suffering from worsening pain.

Before my parents could go to their car, Oma Erika grabbed my father's arm. She told him, with a serious face, something I could not understand. My mother translated, nodding, "Nour and Serhat can't come back to this house anymore!" He glared at my mother for a moment before they silently left the house. I was shocked by the cold manner of discarding. *Why could Nour not return to us? Because of her in-laws only? Why were Oma Erika and my mother so decisively against her? What would happen with Nour now? Would we see each other again?*

Beginning of November 1991

On the day of Nour's release, my mother went to Oslar hospital with Onkel Walter, who had come with a transporter that was loaded with used furniture for Nour's new apartment.

I was with Mamun and Alim on the veranda when they informed me about her move. They also said that my parents were still disappointed with Nour's decision. "She was only 17 years old when she ran away and secretly met with Ammu Serhat," Alim said. Mamun added, "And when our parents heard about it from other people, Nour and Ammu Serhat had to marry to safeguard our reputation even though Ammu Serhat didn't have a high standing as we had." I could not understand my parents' attitude. *How could these be good reasons to condemn her?*

Still, Nour, Ammu Serhat, and *Rahila,* my newborn niece, moved into an apartment in Oslar, while my parents and Oma Erika forbade us to visit them. I felt confused and insecure. After we had lost so much in the war, I had believed that at least our family would stay together. In reality, however, the elders decided to break close contact with Nour. For the first time, I doubted if I could always count on my family. *What would happen if I broke their rules? Would they also abandon me?*

A few days after Nour had moved in her apartment, my father flew back to Mosul. Once again, I was afflicted by fears. *Would I ever see him again? Would I ever see Manal again? How long would we stay in Amtal? When would we move again? Could we finally settle somewhere? Who would be there for me then? Would my family be united again?*

III. Kastel

November 1991-March 1992

"Application for negative certification"

Thursday, November 21, 1991

Tap tap tap ding zip tap tap ... Onkel Walter was sitting at his desk under a yellow table lamp. His face was tense. Dozens of cigarette butts filled the ashtray next to his typewriter. Between piles of folders, he was typing a letter to the Society of St. Pius[28], which had put up a house in Kastel for sale. He signed the purchase contract at the end of August, intending to rent out the house to us and help us settle in Kastel. He and my parents favored Kastel over Amtal since its infrastructure was much more developed.

When the Kasteler town council found out, however, that my family was planning to move in Paul-Ehrlich-Straße[29] 4, it decided to block our efforts.

> I would like to inform you that the Kasteler town council made use of their right of preemption, which means they aim to buy your property for "infrastructural reasons" even though a private person, me, already signed a purchase agreement.
>
> The case was already discussed at two town council meetings. Prior to the first meeting, my lawyer, the vice mayor, and I met in the town hall to a) let the town council know about the reasons for my purchase, hoping they would give up the

---

28 a Roman-Catholic priestly fraternity
29 name of a street (*Straße*)

right of preemption and b) explain the urgency of the case and its legal uncertainty.

After the first town council meeting, I was informed by a letter to abide by the deadline in case I wanted to object to the town council's decision. My lawyer thus sent a request for a negative certification to the town on October 28, 1991. Consequently, the case was discussed on another town council meeting on November 6, 1991. Before the second meeting was held, the Catholic pastor of Kastel called the vice mayor, at my request, and recommended the selling in our interest.

When I called the mayor after the second meeting, he told me that the town council decided to let the Mühlheimer State Association of Towns and Municipalities investigate the case "due to the problem of asylum seekers." I told him that I could not understand the determination to only give up the right of preemption if it was legally enforced. Moreover, I told him that my sister was not an asylum seeker, anyway, but in urgent need to find a place for her four children who would soon be naturalized. He told me, once more, that her social situation was irrelevant.

I assume that the town council, knowing that they are in an indefensible legal position, engages the higher authority in Mühlheim to receive a superior affirmation that they cannot create any housing space for asylum seekers, which they claim they do not have. This way, they almost certainly also intend to counter future allocation of asylum seekers by higher government agencies.

Two years ago, the town council a) sold a house that was inhabited by a Turkish family to a company that tore it down to build owner occupied flats. The company owner's wife is a party member of the Christian Democratic Union (CDU) and of the town council and b) sold a house that was inhabited by asylum seekers to a third person who forced the residents, per lawsuit, to leave the house for personal use. There might be even more current cases.

With this knowledge, one needs to try hard not to lose one's self-control. I thus intend to continue in the legal way. My sister and her four children will move into Paul-Ehrlich-Straße 4 tomorrow, November 22, 1991, as we agreed upon on the telephone.

The commitment for a mortgage loan has already been issued. Due to the delay, which has been caused by the Kasteler town council, the transfer of property could not take place yet. This, however, is the condition for the payout. Based on our purchase agreement of August 28, 1991, the right of withdrawal can be exercised if the purchase price (150,000 DM) is not paid by December 1, 1991. I assume that the

```
legal inquiry will lead to a verdict in our favor,
so that the payout can follow soon. In the meantime,
I will pay the interest on which we agreed. I hope
for your accordance. Respectfully, ...
```

Friday, November 22, 1991

We left Amtal after lunch under a blue sky. When we arrived in Kastel, the sky was covered with gray clouds. We got out of the car and stepped on a narrow sidewalk. A cold wind was blowing through the street. I was freezing even though I was wearing Alim's old, gray pullover.

"That is it!" my mother said, pointing at a dirty, yellowed house. Moss beset the pitched roof. The front garden hedge had wildly shot up. I was skeptical. *That condemned house?*

Wary, I followed my family. We entered the property through an olive corroded metal door on concrete slabs that were largely covered with dark brown soil. The front garden largely consisted of dirt. "Your uncle cleared out all the rotten trees," my mother said before she led us around the house under barren grape vines, which hung down from a gray corroded metal frame. Two tall trees had grown in the backyard, one in front of a garage, the other one next to it. "A cherry and a plum tree," she said. It was the first plum tree I had seen, and it was a huge one. Its thick, dark brown trunk covered the gray light post of the street behind our backyard. Looking around with a half-open mouth, I noticed that no tree in our garden held a single leave. *It almost looked like the dead place around*

Sheikh Ibrahim, only in darker tones. I looked into the overcast sky. An airplane was flying over us. Suddenly, war pictures flashed through my mind. I was horrified.

"Yallah, we go inside," Mamun told me. I followed them back to the entrance door. While my mother looked for the keys in her purse, cars passed by behind us. Beyond, I heard the horn of a train. The railway station was next to our house. Kastel was much louder than Amtal. *Would the inside of the house also be different from Oma Erika's house?* I wondered.

When we entered the house, I was crushed by a constricted space. "It was built in 1954 and has 775 square feet," my mother said. The hallway was covered with brown linoleum, the surrounding walls with dark brown wood panels. A filthy olive carpet was glued on the stairs that led to the second floor. The living room in front of us contained the same carpet. We passed a tiny, foul guest bathroom before we entered through a rusty doorframe a small kitchen. White, wooden cupboards stood around, unarranged. "I painted them when your father looked after you," she said. "The windows are only single-glazed but have shutters," she continued, half-content. Silent, we followed her to the living room, which was relatively spacious. She opened a squeaky glass door to the veranda. Once more, I looked at the fallow garden—disappointed. *This house was not at all like Oma Erika's or Onkel Walter's house! Moreover, it was even much further away from what we used to have in Mosul—a home.*

"Let me show you the sleeping rooms and the bathroom upstairs," my mother said. Only after she had said these words did I realize that we did not have to flee anymore. *We finally had our own house again.* Suddenly, I felt relieved, even curious and excited to inspect the rooms upstairs.

Sophia and I went ahead to the second floor on squeaky stairs. The three bedrooms contained a gray, rough carpet, yellowed wallpaper, and an old gas heater. The bathroom was tiled gray. Some tiles were broken. The bathtub was yellowed and scratched, the silicone joints mildewed; but I accepted it, thankful that the toilet did not stink as much as the one downstairs.

When we went back to the first floor, my mother opened the basement door in the hallway. We followed her on narrow, concrete stairs. "The walls consist of World War II ruins," she said. Facing a high humidity and spooky dark shades around us, the word "war" made me feel even tenser. Only the staircase had concrete flooring. The other three rooms had a moldy soil. The ceilings were low. I felt crushed again. *What a stifling place!*

Fortunately, we soon walked back to the living room, which by then was filled with a strange smell. "What's that?" I pulled up my nose. "It's the gas heater. It leaks. I turned it on before we went upstairs," my mother said. I learned that gas smelled like rotten eggs. "Go collect our bags from the car and the two mattresses. We'll sleep in the living room tonight. We can't afford to heat all of the rooms," she said. We did what we were told.

That night, I slept soundly, thankful that we finally settled somewhere even though I knew that so much had to be done to transform this house into a home.

Monday, November 25, 1991

After the question of Paul-Ehrlich-Straße 4 had been discussed in a third town council meeting, the mayor called Onkel Walter. He told him that the town council decided to give up the right of preemption and issue the negative certification in the course of the week.

Wednesday, December 4, 1991

Since the negative certification was not issued as it had been promised, Onkel Walter called the mayor, who promised that a messenger would deliver the document by December 6. When Onkel Walter blamed him for being responsible that the seller had gained the right to withdraw from the contract due to this delay, the mayor hung up without a word.

The town of Kastel tried every trick not to provide my family housing.

Mid-December 1991

Kastel was a conservative town, led by the CDU. It counted about 10,000 inhabitants that predominantly belonged to the white middle class. Further, about 130 asylum seekers, largely coming from North Africa and the Middle East, lived in small metal trailer homes at the town border. Not only were they physically segregated, like in many towns; they were also put in emotional distress since they were denied a working permit and often only given a temporary suspension of deportation.

Around Paul-Ehrlich-Straße, my siblings and I stuck out with our darker skin and black hair. I did not notice the difference—until we were treated differently. Our neighbors greeted each other every day when they collected their mail. When we greeted them, they stared at us or turned around as if we did not exist. It bothered me with questions and feelings of inadequacy. *Why did they reject us?*

The Hoyerswerda riots of September 1991 marked the beginning of small, but violent civil unrests against immigrants in Germany, which was not only struggling with increasing numbers of asylum seekers but also with the political challenges and economic costs of its reunification. After we had collected a television from other people's bulky garbage on a sidewalk one night, we repeatedly saw burning asylum seeker houses and injured non-white people on the news. The people that were attacked often looked like us. The situation frightened me. *Would we soon be attacked as well?*

One afternoon, we walked to the town center when a middle-aged couple approached us from the distance. As they came closer, they crossed the street to the other side. While the woman whispered something to the man, both glared at us with judging eyes. All of a sudden, 3-year-old Sophia shouted, "Ausländer raus!" ("Foreigners out of here!"), the first slogan she had learned in Germany. Mamun quickly held his hands over her mouth while the couple kept glaring. I was scared they would come over and harm us. *Fortunately, they let us walk away.*

Still, the hostilities we faced increasingly made me feel alienated. I questioned my identity. I felt unsure of myself. I wondered, *What is suddenly so wrong with us? And who are we in the eyes of those Germans? Monsters?*

The more I thought about it, the more I adopted the thought that something could indeed be wrong with us.

Wednesday, January 29, 1992

While I spent most of the time with my siblings at home, the legal battle against the town continued. Onkel Walter's lawyer sent a letter to the town council, requesting to issue the negative certification by February 4, 1992. He also threatened to make an administrative claim against the town in case of a further delay.

The town council kept us in limbo the entire time.

Beginning of February 1992

My mother did not talk with us about our problematic social situation. She was hardly at home anyway since she worked three jobs to feed us and pay the rent. Still, we increasingly felt her anger and despair.

She would leave in the early mornings to work as a cashier in a bakery and come back around noon. In time, she more and more often entered the house like a bomb. When we left a coloring book on the table or another trace somewhere, she would chase us through the house and shout at us. "You're nothing but a catastrophe. What have I done to deserve you?" The more often she said these words, the more I felt like a useless burden on her and the more I tried to satisfy her. Yet, even when we had cleaned the house and had done all the chores she had given us, she often looked at us as if all our work was not good enough. Stressed, she would run to the basement, cook, and call us to collect the food. She rarely sat down with us to eat together, and soon we gave up asking her if she would. *Maybe she didn't want to lose her authority. Maybe she was too tired to show a lot of interest in us. Maybe she was completely overwhelmed.* Either way, we tried to say just as little in her presence and do what she expected to not burden her.

After lunch, she would go to the bakery again. Around 7 p.m., she would come back. She would stand at the sink in our kitchen, quickly eat a piece of bread with spreads, and leave again to clean a medical office. Sometimes, she went to the medical office directly from the bakery. Twice a week, she also did a paper route from 9 to 11 p.m. We thus went to bed alone. Even when she was at home, she would not sing us goodnight songs like in Mosul, or hug and kiss us. Instead, she would send us to bed by a tired command. I missed her affection. I increasingly felt abandoned and wondered, *Did she not love us anymore? Why? What did we do wrong?*

One day, it was around noon, we were watching television when she suddenly entered the living room. We did not hear her open the front door. "I work day and night and you useless guys watch television?" she shouted. Mamun switched off the television at once. She ran back to the hallway where she saw my shoes in front of the shoe rack, came back, grabbed my arm, and dragged me along! "Please, what have I done?" I dared to ask. I knew what was going to happen again. She threw me in front of the rack and shouted, "I told you to put your shoes inside the rack!" Next, she reached out and slapped my cheek full force with her flat hands: left, right, left, again and again, before she finally stopped and disappeared to the kitchen. The pain I felt was immeasurable. I had never been beaten in Iraq. My body was shaking from terror. Tears were rolling down my cheeks while I stared at the brown linoleum, inconsolable. *Why?*

The injustices we experienced outside fed the violence inside my family.

From the day we had moved to Kastel, my mother started attacking us more and more often. Soon, I was more and more in fear when she was at home. My security depended on her moods. Still, none of my siblings was beaten as often I was. Mamun and Alim remained an alliance like in Iraq. They also grew stronger physically every month. Mamun fulfilled the role of an overseer for us. Thus, he was not targeted. Alim was slapped a few times, but he knew how to appease her. He learned to play the flute at school and played it at home every time she asked for it. Sophia was slapped more often and yet not as frequently as I was. She carried a German forename. She was my mother's last hope. *She was supposed to become what my brothers and I couldn't— German.* Still, her skin was also somewhat brown, and I assumed that *she would have similar difficulties to be accepted in Kastel.*

Sunday, March 1, 1992

The telephone rang in the evening. I picked it up, "Sultan."

"Habibi, how are you? What are you doing? I miss you a lot," *my father* said.

It was almost a miracle when the telephone lines to Iraq were open.

My heartbeat raced immediately, "Baba! When do you come to Germany?"

"Inshallah soon. Your mother told me she has been looking for a kindergarten place for you for four months, but no one wants to take you. I hope she finds a place soon."

"I don't need any kindergarten. When you come, we can just go for a walk," I said.

"Yes, habibi, we'll do that," he paused. "Do you listen to your mother?"

I wanted to tell him how mean she had become, but then I just said, "Yes." I had promised him to listen to her, and for some reason I believed that *things would become better.*

Monday, March 2, 1992

My mother introduced us to carnival. Since we did not celebrate carnival in Iraq, she explained the tradition before we went to my aunt to get the things we needed. "People dress up in costumes and have fun together," she said, making us curious. At my aunt's, we borrowed costumes and make-up. Mamun and Alim painted their face white; Sophia got a pink princess's dress, while my mother made a clown of me. She painted my face white, my nose red, and draw three red teardrops on my cheek. A red hat almost covered my black hair. We were ready to go.

The gymnasium was already packed with people when we arrived. Some were dressed up. Some just dyed their hair in neon colors. Most families were sitting at tables, eating sausages and drinking soft drinks. My mother led us to a free table next to the stage. We sat down, quietly. Everything felt strange, especially the silence at our table. Most people were chatting and laughing. Some gazed at us, while I felt out of place. *Did I look stupid?*

"You can eat or drink something over there," my mother told us. Knowing that we could not afford the expensive food outside, we politely said, "No." When we looked around with big eyes, she gave me a 2 DM coin, "Just go like the other kids and get something to eat." I got up and walked to the food counter, wearing my red, silk clown costume. Many people looked at me. No one was so perfectly dressed up, and I felt like a real clown—sad and alone. No one talked to me, and I did not dare to approach anyone either since I knew that my

German was insufficient. Fear of rejection made me walk back to my family. *They were everything I had.*

Friday, March 6, 1992

In the end, our survival struggles in the aftermaths of the war led to some successes. My family, except my father and Manal, had escaped to a war-free country. We settled in a house. A few neighbors started to respond to our greetings in a friendly way. We were naturalized. We received full healthcare. My mother earned some money. We could afford simple but good food. Still, fighting continued on other frontiers. Reaching to be accepted in Kastel was not an easy battle; and even though I did not feel very close to Onkel Walter, I was glad that he supported us in this battle. He typed another letter to the town council, expressing his consternation about the council's attempts to chase my family away.

> I want to express my disappointment at the town council's decision to make use of the right of preemption after I had informed you about my sister's situation. Your decision lacked any legal basis. Still, it took you more than five months to adhere to the law and issue the negative certification. Further, it needs to be noted that a town council, led by the CDU, did not help my sister, who flew from war-torn Iraq and, instead of acting in the Christian command of love, tried to get in

the way through a dubious administrative behavior. Thanks to the Society of St. Pius, the purchase agreement is still valid. After having experienced this arbitrariness, I want to let you know that I still cannot believe that all members of the town council back up this practice. Respectfully,...

III. Kastel

March 1992-August 1993

"Finally, we have you back"

End of March 1992

I HAD JUST FINISHED EATING my breakfast cereal when my mother told me with a contented smile, "You'll start kindergarten today." Surprised by the promising news, I smiled back. Finally, her desperate search had been successful. I was glad and hopeful for the both of us. *Me being accepted for kindergarten could release some pressure off her and improve my security at home.*

It would take years before she would tell me that, for five months, all three kindergartens of Kastel preferred German-speaking children to me. Her bakery colleagues had repeatedly told her that their children had gotten a kindergarten place without delay.

At last, the Catholic kindergarten at the small Goldbach River accepted me, which brought a series of positive changes into my life.

Around 9 a.m., my mother took me along to the one-story, flat-roofed building. Only few buildings in Kastel held a flat roof. I was attracted by the construction. It reminded me of the houses in Mosul. Excited but also nervous about starting kindergarten, I followed her into the entrance hall. A middle-aged woman approached us. She exchanged a few words with my mother, who then ran on to work. For a second, I felt deserted, until the woman kneeled down. She took me by the hand and said with a gentle smile, "Willkommen, Junis! Ich bin Bärbel." *Bärbel, my new kindergarten teacher, seemed to be a friendly person.* I felt in safe hands.

She led me down a long corridor along some shoe racks. Some shoes were orderly put inside the shoe rack; some were lying in front of it, I noticed. We stopped in front of a door that held a cardboard bear. "Du kommst in die Bärengruppe," she said. I looked at her with large, alert eyes, aware that I did not fully understand her. *My German was still too poor.*

Since we had moved to Kastel, I did not hear and speak a lot of German. My mother worked most of the time, and if she was at home, she did not speak much. Mamun and Alim, on the other hand, attended middle school in Kastel and preferred Arabic when they were at home since they were still insecure in German. Sophia did not speak much at all.

I felt troubled. *Would I understand the other children? Would they understand me? Would I make friends? Or would I end up like Mamun and Alim on their first school day in Oslar?*

Either way, I wanted to seize the chance to find a friend. Hopeful, I followed Bärbel into the room. She approached two boys at a table and said, "Ich habe einen neuen Freund für euch. Er heißt Junis. Er spricht kaum Deutsch, aber er ist sehr nett. Kann er bei euch sitzen?" The boys nodded and pulled back a chair for me. I sat down and shyly looked around. The two boys had blonde hair, like most children in the room. Only three boys looked similar to me. They were playing by themselves. Some other children were drawing at group tables. Some were sitting in the corner browsing books and talking with each other.

"Er ist Dominik und ich bin Marcus," *Marcus* said.

"Und wie heißt du?" *Dominik* asked me.

I kept silent, afraid to make a mistake.

Shortly, Bärbel called from behind, "Er heißt Junis. Spielt einfach mit ihm!"

"Willst du mit uns auf dem Teppich mit Autos spielen?" Dominik asked.

Since I knew that "spielen" meant playing, I nodded.

We got up and began to play on a carpet with matchbox-cars.

For two hours, we pushed the cars to each other with excited faces and energized bodies, repeatedly laughing and impressed by the speed of the cars. Once again I noticed, *Having fun didn't depend on language.*

Sunday, April 19, 1992

Two challenging and exhilarating kindergarten weeks passed quickly. I needed some days to, time and again, overcome my fear of making mistakes and see that I could have a pleasant time with most children without speaking perfect German. Still, I learned German quickly, mostly by playing with the other children. Moreover, our teachers sang Easter songs with us every day since Easter drew near. I was eager to learn more about it.

On Easter Sunday morning, my family and I left Kastel to visit Oma Erika and celebrate Easter together. After our two-hour drive, we exited the freeway at Lutterberg and drove down meandering streets in the midst of the Solling uplands. Once again, I marveled at the green forest, which was dominated by spruces and beeches as I could now tell after I had learned their names at kindergarten. Entranced, I opened the window and inhaled the fresh forest air.

When we entered the first village, I spotted bushes decorated with colored eggs in people's gardens. Never before had I seen how Easter was celebrated in Germany. My mother saw Sophia's and my enthusiastic faces in the driving mirror. She was pleased about it. She stopped on a side street and took a picture of us in front of a decorated bush.

Around noon, we parked on Oma Erika's driveway. Oma Erika opened the front door before we could ring the bell. *She was awaiting us.* She gave me a kiss on my cheek and a warm hug. I felt happy. *In Amtal, everything was good.* My mother wouldn't beat me because Oma Erika wouldn't allow it, I knew. Cheerful, I kissed and hugged her back.

We gathered in the kitchen. Oma Erika showed us the colored eggs she had bought for our egg hunt in the garden. Before we went outside, she led us to the veranda, where she had already served venison goulash, red cabbage, and bread dumplings. She always cooked the freshest, most delicious food for us. I was under a spell in her presence.

After we had indulged ourselves, my siblings and I waited in the kitchen while my mother hid the eggs in the garden. I was agog and ready for the hunt. Soon, she joyfully called from the backyard, "You can come out now."

For some reason, she behaved differently in Amtal. She seemed to be more comfortable with herself, and she was kind and generous to us. I was glad about it. We ran outside—laughing, dashing in different directions, and trying to find the eggs. *Easter was fun. Easter was peace.* I wished every day could be like Easter.

JUNE 1992

Unfortunately, not every day compared with Easter. Certain moments in my everyday life still terrified me. The first week after we had moved to Kastel, I ran to the basement for dear life and hid between the freezer and the gas oven when the Civil Defense siren started at noon. Even 16 months after the Second Gulf War my heart still began to race when I heard a siren. Strangely, I was still nervous even though I knew I was safe. The war, the terror, the death from above were still ingrained in my mind.

Accordingly, airplanes frightened me as well. I did not talk about it. I drew it. During the first months in kindergarten, my pictures showed warplanes, tanks, bombs, broken houses, and dead people lying on bloodstained streets. Bärbel was very attentive. She carefully talked with me about every picture. She told me that what we had experienced was very bad and that she was glad that we were in Germany and safe now.

Over time, my pictures became free of blood. Still, they were far from peace. Some pictures still contained random war elements, as if the war was following my family and me to Germany.

July 1992

Friends helped me overcome my war traumas. By July 1992, *Marcus, Dominik, and I had become good friends.* In addition to kindergarten, we often met in our free time. Dominik lived nearby. I visited him almost every day. Usually, Marcus joined us playing. That summer, we discovered the best hiding places in the thicket. "Ready or not, here I come!" one of us would yell, while the others were hiding in the bushes next to the railway track, silently observing the seeker and, if necessary, quietly changing positions. The more exciting and happy moments we shared together, the more my war memories were pushed away. In addition, I was learning German at a high speed in their presence and with their support.

By July 1992, my siblings and I had switched to speaking German only at home. We helped each other learn the language. When my mother was at home, she corrected us as well. We still struggled to use the defined and undefined articles correctly, but we got better every day. *Skill comes with practice,* Oma Erika used to say, and I learned that she was right.

Saturday–Wednesday, August 22–26, 1992

We silently followed the news, "Several hundred rioters, partly self-confessed neo-Nazis, attacked an agency and a home for asylum seekers in Rostock Lichtenhagen with Molotov cocktails. About 3,000 applauding Germans attended the mob. The police backed down. The riot went on until it finally fizzled out." While I assumed that my family would be immersing into the German society, I was afraid for our security every time I received these kinds of news reports. *The widespread fear and hate did not seem to differentiate between asylum seekers and immigrants.* Some Germans targeted people who simply looked different—believing in contradictory pseudo-justifications I did not understand. As if asylum seekers and immigrants took away all the jobs. As if "they" lived a lazy and luxury life, paid by the taxpayers. As if "they" were uncivilized and dangerous. And so on.

Mid-September 1992

A few weeks after I had been admitted to kindergarten, Sophia also got a place. She attended the neighboring group in my corridor—the dinosaurs.

Usually, Mamun and Alim picked us up from kindergarten at 1:30 p.m.

One day, on our way home, we passed a house that had a Great Dane lying in the driveway behind a metal fence. A boy my age was standing close by. He looked over us for a second before he shouted to his dog, "Attack! Foreigners." The dog jumped up, hit the fence with his forepaws, and barked loudly. Standing next to Sophia, I held my breath and froze. Mamun grabbed our hands and rapidly crossed the street with us. We walked away, scared and speechless.

Soon, my fright turned into embarrassment. *Why did he despise us if he didn't even know us? Why did some people still not see us as their neighbors, or at least as harmless strangers?*

Sunday, September 20, 1992

In contrast to the fear of random attacks when being outside, our life at home contained a lot of routine. Even Sundays were a strictly run working day. My mother let us sleep until 9 a.m.

After breakfast, we cleaned the house until noon. Usually, I had to clean the bathrooms. After lunch, we continued cleaning before we met for tea at 3 p.m. After tea, we continued to clean the house. Every Sunday was usually the same.

One Sunday, however, my mother allowed us to join an event in the Kasteler Freizeitpark[30]. Clubs, church communities, schools, and kindergartens introduced themselves. The event was opened with a show of the Kasteler band. Surprised, I spotted *Piero,* a kindergarten friend of mine. He was wearing a red felt uniform and a white pair of gloves. We briefly smiled at each other before he started to play his horn with full confidence. The music got under my skin. I got goose bumps. 14 people were playing horns; four people were on troop drums; and one young man played a snare drum that was leading the rhythm with a free and decisive beat. I, too, wanted to learn to play one of these instruments.

After the 15-minute show, Piero directly came to me. He was grinning all over his face and so was I. He gave me his horn to try playing. As I did, his father walked up to us.

"Not bad! You should join us, boy. You could play the horn, like Piero," he told me.

"I'd love to, but I have to ask my mother. It's expensive, isn't it?" I said.

"Na, you're a kid. For you it's 40 DM a year. If I can pay it, your mother can pay it, too. If you come, I'll take care of you

---

30 a recreational park with a swimming pool

like my son. Let me introduce you to my cousin, our maestro. He will explain everything to you," he said.

When he laid his warm hand on my shoulder, I knew I absolutely wanted to become a member of that band. *They seemed to be like a huge family.*

My siblings and I went home late afternoon. Since I knew about our scarce financial resources, I hesitated to share my wish with my mother. At bedtime, however, I dared to approach her. I told her that I would be happy if she allowed me to join the Kasteler band. She looked at me, deliberated for a moment, and then simply said, "Okay." I was surprised. I thanked her and smiled like a 6-year-old who enjoyed his childhood.

Monday, September 21, 1992

At 7 p.m. I met Piero and *Luigi,* his younger brother, in front of the "Clubhaus"[31] in Weinbergstraße, close to my mother's bakery. We went inside the building. As we entered a smoke-filled rehearsal room, I looked around. Except for Piero, Luigi, and me, all club members were adults. Many were drinking beer. I was alarmed. *No one in my family drank alcohol. It was haram—forbidden—*my father used to say. For a second, I felt as if I should not be there. But then, all the club members approached me with a smile and introduced themselves. Some hugged me. Some were relatives of Piero, some

---

31 place/house were the members of a club meet

local Kastelers. I felt warmly welcomed. *Antonio,* the maestro, bought me a Fanta at the counter before he announced, "I'm proud that young kids like Junis join us." Next, he handed me an instrument, "This horn is yours now. You can take it home and practice." The club members clapped their hands, excited. I beamed with joy. It felt like *belonging to a second family,* a family that appreciated me and wanted me to thrive and become successful.

Monday, November 23, 1992

My siblings and I watched the evening news in our living room, "Two neo-Nazis attacked two houses in Mölln, Schleswig-Holstein, in which Turkish families lived. Molotov cocktails were thrown. The 10-year-old, Yaliz Arslan, the 14-year-old, Ayse Yilmaz, and their 51-year-old grandmother, Bahide Arslan, were killed in the flames. During the firefighting operation, the police received several responsibility calls, which ended with 'Heil Hitler.' "

We looked at each other, taken aback. Thoughts flooded my mind. *The poor family! Their poor relatives!* I did not understand. *Why did those hate crimes repeatedly occur in Germany? Was it really all about outward appearances? We looked like Turks, too! We lived in a house, too!* I was horrified.

The news anchor continued, "The number of Germans supporting the 'Ausländer-raus-end-solution' dropped from 50 % to 33 % after the killings." Still, the number did not take away my fear of being targeted in the future again and maybe even in a deadly way. Slowly, a thought I had had before on similar occasions recaptured my mind. *What if we just tried harder to be like Germans? Would we be accepted and safe?*

MID-DECEMBER 1992

I was willing to do anything to be accepted and safe. *My mother knew what I had to do,* I thought. *She was born German,* and I trusted her instructions.

At the beginning of December, my mother asked Sophia and me to act in a play in kindergarten. Sophia was wrapped in a white cloth, playing Maria. I was standing behind a crèche with a stick in my hand, playing a shepherd who came to see newborn Jesus. Bärbel had read the story of Jesus to us two weeks earlier. Until then, I had not heard about "God's son." In Iraq, I had been told about Allah and the Prophet Muhammad. I felt confused initially, but willingly accepted the ideological shift. In fact, I enjoyed our common play experience.

After the play, parents congratulated us for the good show. I appreciated their recognition and felt as if I was on the right path of being accepted by others and safe.

SUNDAY, DECEMBER 13, 1992

We watched the evening news, "300,000 people marched in Hamburg with candles in their hands against xenophobia and for more tolerance. Marches are planned for Würzburg, Nuremberg, Stuttgart, Hanover, Leipzig, Frankfurt, Berlin, and more cities." The people's devotion to stop the violence moved me and gave me hope. Yet, I still did not feel safe in my skin in Germany. Like many times before, I prayed my father would come and protect us.

Mid-February 1993

Two wishes became true within two months. First, Oma Erika, Nour, and my mother unexpectedly reconciled for some reasons I was not told. On Christmas Eve 1992, Oma Erika, Nour, *Ammu Serhat,* and Rahila suddenly stood at our front door, smiling and holding presents in their hands. They were part of our family again. I felt overjoyed about our reunification. Second, my father retired in Iraq to come and stay with us in Germany. Discreetly, he had arranged a successor for his posts. A sudden escape with us to Germany in 1991 would have put all of us in danger since it would have been seen as treason by Saddam Hussein.

On his arrival day, we drew a welcome home poster and put it on our cupboard in the living room, "Endlich haben wir dich wieder," ("Finally, we have you back.") We also put flowers, candles, coffee, and pastries on the dining table. Onkel Walter, my aunt, *Tante Ursula,* and my cousins, *Moritz* and *Sabrina,* came as well to welcome him.

We were overwhelmed with joy when my father arrived. My mother was smiling, too. Yet, he had difficulties recognizing her. Sometimes, he even stared at her. She had hollow cheeks, tired eyes, and completely gray hair by then. Before we started to eat, he took a deep breath. He raised his eyebrows and said in English, "God knows I would have done anything to spare us this painful experience, but now we're in security at last." Onkel Walter nodded. My father looked at us and repeated his words in Arabic. Mamun and Alim nodded, while Sophia and I just looked at him. We already had difficulties understanding Arabic. Since we had entered kindergarten, we only heard and spoke German. I suddenly felt deeply troubled. *I had learned German, but I hardly understood my father now.*

Beginning of March 1993

After kindergarten, I now spent the afternoons mostly at home to help my father learn German and orient himself. Plenty of challenges awaited us. His new job was to manage our household and support us. However, he struggled to meet his new challenges. He did not know how to cook, how to do the washing, how to dress us, how to get things done in the German health care system, and much more. Many things that were important to find his way were new and strange to him. He did not talk much, except apologizing for making mistakes. Soon, I often found him sitting in the living room, staring outside the window with a sad face and tears in his eyes. I felt sorry for him. I wanted to help him. Sometimes, I could convince him to go outside with me for a walk.

Beginning of summer 1993

One night, my father called us to the living room. He announced, "I need to speak with your mother tonight, and I want you to say your opinion, too. I don't know what to do. I am exhausted," he said. We nodded and sat down. I felt nervous. *What was I supposed to say?*

When she came from her paper route, he confronted her right away, "Please, sit down. We need to speak. You need to spend more time at home," he said.

She sat down and looked at him as if they had had the same argument many times before. "What do you want?" she asked, irritated.

He raised his voice, "100 DM more a month doesn't make a big difference. Our children need a mother. We need each other. We still have some money in Iraq."

"You can talk. I'm the only one who earns money here! I don't want them to walk around with clothes from the Red Cross[32] anymore. People laugh at us. Don't tell me what they need. I looked after them when you were not here," she shouted at him.

---

[32] German Red Cross Society, third largest Red Cross society in the world, offers a wide range of services within and outside Germany such as care for the elderly, children, and youth

He turned to us, "Tell your mother that she should spend more time at home!"

Yet, we did not dare to say a word. I did not want to take sides. They were both my parents, and I loved both of them and needed to be loved by both of them.

"Go to bed!" my mother told us.

We obeyed.

Upstairs, I lay down and listened to their shouting. Soon, they argued about things that had happened in Iraq. They called each other liar and other names. I felt miserable. *Why were they so mean to each other?*

After their last words, an eerie silence occupied our house. I could not fall asleep from concerns. *Could they solve their problems and reconcile?*

Next morning, Alim asked around if anyone had seen his jeans. We searched the house. Eventually, my mother found them in the lowest drawer of his shelf. She blamed my father, "You didn't put them in the correct place, and you ironed them poorly." He did not say a word. With an angry face, he went down to the kitchen to prepare our lunch boxes. I followed him to help him. Shortly, my mother came after us. She pulled out a knife from the drawer, "You can't even wash the dishes properly. Just leave all housework for me when you are unable to do it correctly!" He beat his fists on his head several times, shouting, "Ya Allah!" I had never seen him like this before. I was scared. *He was not the strong father I used to know. Moreover, my parents did not get along at all, compared to our life in Iraq.*

End of August 1993

It took my parents several months to allocate their new responsibilities in our family and adapt to their new roles. In the end, my father started working as a cashier at nights in the gas station of the Main-Taunus-Zentrum (MTZ), one of the biggest malls in Hesse. He was glad he could support us financially, even if the work itself was a social decline for him. My mother, on the other hand, began a five-year kindergarten teacher's training, which included part-time work in a kindergarten. She enjoyed working with children. Our finances were finally sufficient to get independence from welfare checks.

Not only did we slowly stabilize financially; the relationships in my family improved as well. My father looked after my siblings and me during the day. I felt in safe hands again. He protected us from my mother's rage attacks, which decreased anyway after he had come to Germany and shared the responsibility for us. My mother was more relaxed overall. As a result, I felt more and more comfortable at home.

Moreover, the public attacks on non-white people decreased as well, which generally made me feel safer in Germany even though I still felt the pressure to assimilate.

As the relationships and atmosphere around me developed in positive ways, it was easier for me to focus on myself again. I was looking forward to starting primary school soon.

III. Kastel

September 1993-August 1997

"Rules of the games"

Beginning of September 1993

The kitchen clock showed 7:30 a.m. when my father and I were ready to leave. He walked me to Pestalozzi Schule, my new school. In contrast to my first walk to Bärengruppe, I felt quite confident. *My German was good enough, and Marcus and Dominik would be in my class, too.* I was looking forward to spending the next four years with them.

When we sat down at a group table in our new classroom, we looked around with keen eyes. Our new class had 20 students, and everyone looked excited. Three boys looked similar to me, I noticed, automatically. As our class teacher, *Ms. Schneider,* asked us to introduce ourselves, I got to know their names: *Ricardo, Hakim,* and *Nasir.* The last two names were Arabic, I remembered. Even though I did not know the three boys, it strangely made me feel safer to see that I was not the only one who stuck out with a darker physical appearance and a non-German name.

Tuesday, November 9, 1993

My father already had his jacket on when I came home from school. "I go to the town hall now. I signed up for the election commission of the first Kasteler Council of Foreigners," he said. Since I did not understand what he meant, I asked him to explain it to me. "The Hessian Municipal Code prescribes for every municipality that counts more than 1,000 foreigners to install a council that represents the interests of foreign citizens and advises the town in these matters," he said. I smiled, surprised by the existence of that council and his new involvement in local politics. While he put on his shoes, I asked him for his reasons. "Kastel gave us a home. I want to give something back. In addition, I want to help foreigners have an easier start here," he said. I was impressed by his motivation and his action. He probably saw it in my eyes. "You can visit me with your brothers around 8 p.m.," he said before he left.

We met him in the town hall in the evening. The mayor stepped to the speaker's desk to proclaim the voter turnout, which was 29 %. He congratulated the nine elected representatives, who all had a different migration background. Their families and about 60 Kastelers clapped their hands before everyone bustled around the new representatives. Never before had I seen so many people with diverse skin colors speaking different languages and wearing different kinds and colors of clothes—all gathering peacefully at one place in Kastel. Standing with Mamun, Alim, and my father in the midst of all people, my eyes were wide open. *We all looked different, and still, we were the same, just people who lived together in one community.* For the first time, I fully felt like Kastel was my new home, a place where I could connect with people, a place where I could be myself.

BEGINNING OF DECEMBER 1993

When the Christmas season started, Ms. Schneider invited us to a baking event. I was looking forward to our community experience and to learning how to bake Christmas cookies.

We met in the art room. My classmates and I were visibly excited about creating the sweet treasures together. Some parents had come as well to help us in preparing the dough. We rolled it and cut out stars, moons, and hearts, smiling at our common creations and at each other. Every single one of us was important for the success of our common enterprise. I felt as if I belonged.

Friday, July 15, 1994

At the end of the term, my classmates and I waited impatiently at our tables while Ms. Schneider handed out our first report cards. Excited, I went over mine. She assessed my skills and my educational needs in a text; and I was impressed by her knowledge of me.

> School report: Dear Junis, you study diligently. You do your work accurately, most of the time independently, and by now faster. Sometimes, however, you do not complete some tasks or you forget a part of your homework. You should always double-check the assignments. You behave in a companionable, cooperative, and responsible way toward your classmates. You can easily play and work together with other children. You follow the agreed upon rules. It annoys you when other children do not adhere to them. You should try to react a bit more

> calmly to those children. Most of the time, you follow the lessons attentively and with interest. In our narration circle, you are a good listener. You should participate more actively in discussions during the lessons. You have learned reading quickly. You read texts that we have practiced with a good flow and stress, and unknown texts slowly to grasp their meaning. Your printed letters and your cursive are clearly structured and neatly written. If we practice a word, you can write it error-free when dictated. In free writing, you write the words with phonetic accuracy. You complete exercises with numbers up to ten error-free. Sometimes, you use auxiliary material for addition and subtraction exercises with numbers up to 20. With some practice, you will carry out these exercises faster in your head. You show a good feeling for colors and forms in art. In physical education, you quickly grasp motion sequences and the rules of the games.

After school, I showed my parents my report card. They read it, smiled, and congratulated me with kisses on my cheeks. "Good job," they said. I felt happy about their appreciation and, for the first time since we had come to Germany, somewhat proud of my abilities.

August 1994

Like most children at Pestalozzi Schule, I had a diverse circle of friends. Friendship at school often started with common interests. By September, I had become friends with *Jonathan*, a classmate of mine who collected stamps as I did. We often met after school at his big house in front of the strawberry fields. His mother was a psychologist and had her practice in the loft. Jonathan's room was on the second floor. We were often sitting on his beige, fluffy carpet, sorting and trading stamps. In addition to the latest German stamps, I had some from Iraq. My father had given them to me, and I gave some to Jonathan, often in exchange for some old German ones. *Our hobby was fun and for free.*

Sometimes, I also visited Hakim, my other table neighbor. Usually, he did not invite classmates home. His parents hardly spoke German and were shy toward German speaking people, but they made an exception for Nasir and me, *probably because we were of Arab descent.* Hakim lived on the fifth floor in a yellow tower block next the railways, not far from Paul-Ehrlich-Straße. The first time I visited him, I was instantly allured by a spicy odor that escaped from his apartment door. When Hakim led me to the living room, where his family awaited us, I found that the scent came from there. Plates with Kubbah[33] and pots with vegetables had been set on the floor. We sat down on the ground in a circle and began to eat, as my family had done in Sheikh Ibrahim. I was eating Kubbah for the first time since the war, and I remembered the particularly spicy taste. I smiled.

---

33 Arabic, Levantine dish, rice balls filled with spicy ground meat and fresh peppermint

Dinner at Marcus's home was different. His house lay at the Goldbach River. From his living room, we could look through huge windowpanes at the small river while the blue-tiled floor would warm our feet. I only stayed for dinner when his father came home from work late. Marcus, his younger brother, his baby sister, and I would sit at a long table, far away from each other, while his mother would serve us small portions on sterile, white dishes. Dinner usually ended quickly and with no leftovers. At 6:30 p.m. sharp, I had to leave before his father came. "It's time for our family to be together and alone," his mother told me one time. Sometimes, his father came home early. He would then first drive me home before his family had dinner. The rule seemed weird to me at the beginning. *In Iraq, they would have insisted that I stay for dinner and spend time with the entire family,* I thought. Anyway, I quickly adapted to the change. I appreciated Marcus, and I wanted to keep a good relationship with him. The dinner rule was insignificant compared to the joy we shared. That summer, we spent many hours on his garage roof, where we had built our own room with wooden boards. We often sat side by side in our covert space, reading out jokes and laughing from our hearts.

Saturday, February 1995

Since my parents were able to save enough money, we could afford to buy a new couch. We went to the Kasteler home improvement center and bought a dark green leather corner couch. Finally, we didn't have to sit on worn-out couches from the garbage anymore. We celebrated our modernized living room with homemade chocolate cake and tea.

SUMMER 1995

In addition to modernizing our house little by little, we made a new garden, which turned into *a living jungle* in the summer. Our grape vines became an impenetrable blanket of dark green, palm-sized leaves that grew together with our raspberry and blackberry bushes along the mesh wire fence. Together, they created a quiet, shadowy place, where blackbirds would hide from the midday sun. The dense canopy of our cherry tree threw another shadow on our lush lawn, where wild rabbits would graze. Close by, parsley, chives, and rosemary spread a fresh odor underneath our young and thriving mirabelle tree. From all the beauties in our garden, our plum tree remained my favorite. I often climbed it after school, rested on a high branch, and enjoyed some calm time with nature.

When my mother came from her teacher training in the late afternoons, we often began to pick our berries. She would squeeze herself along the bushes and the wire mesh fence, the hard-to-reach part, and pick berries with both hands. Almost never would she put them in the bowl before her hands were fully laden. If one berry jumped out of the bowl, she would put it back right away. Her bowls usually contained so many berries that one more could have brought the entire mountain to fall. *She took a risk, and she was almost always successful.* I admired her skills—her determination, her speed, and her efficiency—and tried to measure up.

Beginning of August 1995

For the first time since we had come to Germany, my family could afford to go on a faraway vacation. Since the Iraqi Dinar[34] slowly regained some value, my father invested some old savings with the help of Onkel Walter at the end of 1993. By 1995, they registered good returns. My father was visibly happy that he could, again, substantially contribute to our financial well-being even though discussions and tensions between him and my mother regarding their new family responsibilities flared up again. Anyway, he bought Onkel Walter's 15-year-old VW Passat for our 600-mile journey to Eraclea Mare, a small coastal town in Northeast Italy. Hikmat, our former family doctor, had invited us. After the war in 1991, Hikmat's family had fled from Mosul to San Dona, a town close to Eraclea Mare. We were looking forward to finally seeing them again.

In the late evening, after our nine-hour trip, we arrived in Eraclea Mare. Hikmat and his family welcomed us at an ice cream parlor with many kisses on our cheeks. We were all smiling, almost nonstop. I was glad to see them again, especially Hikmat. *He was still a cheerful person.*

He exchanged some words with my parents before he looked at me again. "Junis, make the adhan!" he said in Arabic and laughed. It was a joke he used to make since I often called for the prayer when he visited us in Mosul. Yet, I was unable to sufficiently understand and speak Arabic by 1995. I

---

34   currency of Iraq

felt nervous and ashamed of myself. *I owed him my life, but I just looked at him now—speechless, ignorant, and not knowing what to say.*

"Junis and Sophia do not really speak Arabic anymore. We only spoke German with them in the last few years. We wanted them to be successful in school," my father said.

"Oh, okay. Our children speak Italian and Arabic. We wanted them to maintain their language. I think they do okay at school," Hikmat said.

My parents shrugged their shoulders, somewhat embarrassed, before we sat down.

Sophia and I sat down on a white porch swing, while my family and Hikmat's family sat around a table. I listened to their conversation in Arabic, which I hardly understood even though many words sounded somehow familiar. Sometimes, they laughed about old stories while looking at us. I felt deficient and guilty. *I should not have forgotten Arabic.* After four years in Germany, I was separated from former friends, from my past, and from who I used to be. It hurt.

Beginning of September 1995

Back in Kastel, our life continued as usual, except one day when I came home from school and found my parents fighting.

"I thought I'd be safe when I came to Iraq. I thought my husband would stand behind me, but you and your family betrayed me," she shouted.

"When did we betray you? What did we do to you? he shouted back.

"You never intervened when I was suppressed by your family."

"How were you suppressed?"

She remained silent.

Both glared at each other with contempt.

"My only escape was gardening and raising children," she paused. "If my parents had not taught to me otherwise, I'd have not kept the naive faith that our marriage could improve. I'd have divorced you years ago!"

"Alright," my father nodded. "If it was and is so excruciating to live with us, why torture yourself? Go get the divorce!" he said, embittered.

I felt weighed down. Everything I thought I knew about our past was suddenly under heavy attack. *How was she suppressed when we lived like kings in Iraq? What awful things had happened before I was born? What would happen with us now? Would they separate? How would I live as a 9-year-old, depending on parents who had probably never loved each other?* I felt doomed to insecurity.

Mid September 1995

A few days after their quarrel, my mother went to a cure for six weeks. We all met in the living room. With packed bags in her hands, she said, "I need some time on my own. The family stresses me out." No one knew what to say. I still did not understand. *Why were we such a burden on her? Could the doctors help her? Could they help us? Or was my family breaking apart, again?* "See you," she told us with an empty face before she left. I watched her leave, feeling helpless, ashamed, and guilty. *Would she ever really want to see us again after what she had gone through because of us?*

As they drove away, I remembered how she had entered our house that summer, upset and full of shame, "I just heard from a neighbor that everyone thinks that we still live on welfare, that our house, your education, and everything else is paid by the German taxpayers!" The social pressure my mother faced because of us had never really disappeared.

Saturday, January 20, 1996

Life left no recovery time for us. The next problem would even turn into a long battle that would damage us in many respects. When my father came in 1993, our next-door neighbors, an old German couple, all of a sudden stopped talking to us even though we had constantly tried to build a neighborly relationship. Ignoring us was only the beginning of their hostilities. When I came home from school, my father showed me a letter from our neighbors. With a sad face, he asked me to read it.

```
[...] In accordance with the municipal law, quiet
hours have to be respected in any house on work-
ing days from 8 p.m. through 7 a.m. in wintertime.
```

Moreover, it is imperative to adhere to the quiet hours from 1 p.m. through 3 p.m. During that time, people must not be hounded and tormented by noise. On Sundays and on holidays, noise is prohibited 24 hours a day. The municipal law also applies to you and your family.

Children are active and loud. This is understandable and largely tolerated by us. But why do your children have to romp and scream just in the quiet hours? And why do they have to play loud wind instruments just in the quiet hours? Is none of you rational enough to urge your children to be thoughtful?

Last night, the quiet hours were hit hardest. Your children produced so much noise that my wife and I could not listen to our television on room volume at 9 p.m. I called around 10 p.m. and begged your son to make sure it would get quieter. Without any impact. Only by 10:30 p.m. did the penetrating noise in your house and in your veranda stop.

It really cannot go on like this any longer. Have you ever asked yourselves how ruthless your behavior is toward your neighbors? I insistently ask you to adhere to the mandatory rest periods in the future. Respectfully, ...

I put down the letter and looked at him, startled. *How could they call us thoughtless and ruthless when my classmates and their families were much louder at their homes? Did we not have the same rights?* I wondered. Before I could respond, he requested, "You have to write a letter. Your German is better than mine is and better than that of your siblings." I hesitated for a second since I had no idea what to write, but I also felt responsible for my family. *With skills comes responsibility,* I learned. I pulled out a paper from my schoolbag, sat at the kitchen table, and began to write.

> Dear Neighbor, with shock and disappointment, we have read your letter. You will receive a more comprehensive answer when my wife returns from her cure. Thank you. Best regards, ...

Beginning of February 1996

Two days after my mother had returned from her cure, my father called my siblings and me to the living room. He was holding a letter in his hand. "You shall know what is happening between your parents," he said before he began to read it out. In his letter, he told my mother that they would from now on only stay together because we still needed their assistance. He also said that all trust was destroyed because of lies about our life in Iraq, and that they were thus no longer husband and wife. We looked at each other, shattered. Like my mother, he involved us in their conflict. I felt deeply troubled. *Why could they not talk about the past and forgive each other? Why could we not be a normal family with a more or less happy present and future, filled with love and not hate? Why was there only blame and resentment? Why all this destruction and pain?*

Wednesday, July 17, 1996

In contrast to the uncontrollable negativities at home, school was something I could control. School was my opportunity to replace the ongoing misery in my family with some feeling of success. School meant positive challenge: personal development, achievements, and recognition for myself and from others. I thus did not want to just pass the exams. I wanted to become an excellent student. Quantitative grades were introduced in the third school year, and I was looking forward to receiving my report card. I mostly got "As" and some "Bs."

Friday, January 31, 1997

After another successful school term, I had to apply with my midyear report card of the fourth year for middle school. Yet, I was not sure for which school form I should apply.

Aware that I needed advice, I showed my report card to my father and told him that my class teacher recommended me for grammar school, the highest school form.

He looked at me with surprised eyes, "You're the first one among your siblings."

"And the only immigrant of my class, too," I said.

"Be proud!" he said. "I'm sorry I couldn't help you much. But you did it anyway."

Despite his recognition, I still had my doubts if I could be successful at grammar school. *Mamun and Alim went to Realschule, the lower school form, and their grades were average.* "Baba, should I go to grammar school or Realschule?" I asked.

He contemplated for a moment before he said, "Look, son. We lost almost everything in the war, but thank God, we're in Germany, in security. We are privileged to live here. And you are a smart boy. I want you to make this decision on your own."

I was surprised he left this important decision to me even though I was only 10 years old. "In Realschule I'd probably not have to study that hard, and I'd have more free time. In grammar school, I'd have to deal with questions that are more difficult and study much more," I said.

"Yes, but it would be more rewarding, too. Grammar school qualifies you to study at university later," he paused. "I don't worry about you. You can manage grammar school and more. But whatever you decide, I stand behind you," he said.

Friday, February 14, 1997

I reflected on my options for a couple of days before I decided to go to grammar school. *Grammar school was my way to success in life,* I believed. My father was the proof. *If I just studied hard enough, I could also attain the skills to build something good in the future.*

In addition to my promising prospects at school, my parents surprised us with great news. After they had given each other a silent treatment for months, they called us to the kitchen one day to announce that they would extend our house. They showed us the construction plan, which included a front building with a guest bathroom and two shed dormers with two bedrooms, one for them and one for Sophia. "Everyone will have a private room," my mother said, content. We smiled at each other. I assumed that my parents had reconciled. I was hopeful. *If they started such a big project together, they would also plan to stay together as a family.*

Saturday, February 22, 1997

The construction of the shed dormers started in the morning. We observed everything from the Park and Ride[35] behind our backyard. Around noon, the crane juggled roof beams to the opened roof. When Onkel Walter drove along Paul-Ehrlich-Straße, he spotted the construction as well. He parked behind us and rushed to my parents with an angry face. I was alarmed.

"What's happening with my house?" he asked.

"Didn't you tell him?" my father asked my mother.

"No, I didn't find time to talk with him," she said.

"And I've got no time for your silliness. You can't extend the house without informing me. You don't have the right. This is my house!" he shouted at them.

---

35 parking lots with public transport connections

I was taken aback.

My father approached him carefully, "I understand your anger. I thought your sister informed you. Please calm down. What shall we do now?"

"It's too late to talk now." He turned his back on us, got in his car, and drove away.

We looked at each other with big eyes. Each time we made some headway, an obstacle appeared we had to surmount. Yet, I knew that *this problem could only be solved by my parents*.

Friday, May 9, 1997

Late at night, Onkel Walter rang our bell. He handed my father a fat, gray folder. "These documents show how much I spent on Paul-Ehrlich-Straße 4, subtracting the sum of the rent (800 DM per month) which you have paid," he said, tensed up, and left. My father took the folder to our kitchen. We gathered around my parents. When they read aloud the documents, I learned about what Onkel Walter had done before we moved in. He had organized a clearing out. He had installed two new windows, bought insulating material for the loft, had the chimney cleaned, ordered an electrician to build the wires into the wall, and laid tiles in the kitchen. He invested a lot of time and money and recorded every expense.

In 1991, we were thankful for his help. In 1997, we were stunned by his actions. He even put his travel costs and undefined additional costs on a debit note. *In Iraq, his behavior would have been regarded as unusually rude. It was normal that family members helped each other for free. It was a question of honor,* I remembered. I felt disappointed by him.

The last pages of the folder showed four options of how we could purchase the house. The fourth proposal, the cheapest one, supposed a purchase prize that exceeded the sum Onkel Walter paid in 1991 inordinately. My parents were visibly indignant, and I understood, *money can make relationships unbelievably strained and strange.*

Mid-May 1997

The conflict with Onkel Walter led to new conflicts between my parents. Sometimes, they were inaccessible and lost in thoughts, but more often, they yelled at each other. Still, they did not how we could purchase the house, and I was worried we could suffer a financial crisis again.

To distract myself from my fear of possibly suffering from poverty again, I began to write a fictional picture story that would receive the title "A Free Trip to Arabia."

By 1997, however, my Arabic roots were so torn and diffused that I seemed strange to myself. Even though I forgot to speak Arabic, and even though Iraq was largely out of my mind, my roots were still a part of me. For many Germans who did not know me I obviously remained a "foreigner," while my sense of being an Iraqi had dwindled to a vague, romantic idea mixed with Walt Disney imaginations of deserts with cactus, flying carpets, and magic lamps.

WEDNESDAY, JULY 23, 1997

I received my final report card. Even though most of my grades were excellent, I suddenly doubted my achievement. *My grades were the reason why I'd lose some of my friends* who our teachers recommended to lower school forms.

Performance differences had already become apparent in the third school year when grades were introduced. Except for art, music, and physical education (PE), all other grades more or less depended on the German language skills. Some students mastered the German language well and got good grades. Others, especially the socially disadvantaged and/or immigrants, got in most subjects "Cs" or "Ds," which our teachers told us would not suffice to get their grammar school recommendation after the first term of the fourth school year.

Problematically, many teachers applied unfair double standards in the end. Some "Cs" turned out to be good enough for German students that had well-educated parents, while less-educated and/or immigrant parents were not considered a good enough support for their children with respect to the study requirements at grammar school. For students like me, a "B" was thus the minimal requirement to receive a grammar school recommendation.

I felt sorry for Hakim, Nasir, and Ricardo. *Their life was almost ruined at the age of 10.* Their grades did not qualify them for grammar school. Hakim was recommended for Hauptschule, the lowest school form. His future chances to earn enough money for a decent life were scarce, we knew. Only a very few Hauptschüler reached university in Germany after long and onerous educational detours. Hakim's grades reflected his struggles to learn in a system that did not sufficiently support the development of his German language skills. Nasir and Ricardo were recommended for Realschule. Their chances were somewhat better, we knew. With a good leaving certificate, they could do the Abitur[36] at some schools.

Still, I felt like a traitor, knowing that I would be able to study and probably have a good-paying job later, while they principally missed their chance being only 10 years old. I looked at Hakim, concerned.

"Don't worry, Junis. We'll stay friends," he said.

"Of course," I said even though I was afraid to lose contact with him.

Strangely, I also admired him. Even though he was recommended for Hauptschule, he could understand his relatives and friends and speak with them fluently, while I couldn't. *Instead, I'd probably be the only immigrant in my new class at grammar school, and I'd probably have to assimilate even more to succeed.* The more I thought about it, the more I wondered, *Would I lose the last bits of my "Iraqiness" at grammar school?*

August 1997

After my father had scraped his savings together in Iraq, and after we had received an owneroccuoied housing allowance,

---

[36] university-preparatory school leaving qualification in Germany

we were able to overcome the financial hurdle Onkel Walter had given us. We purchased the house in Paul-Ehrlich-Straße and became home owners. Moreover, my mother successfully completed her teacher training. Her new full-time position at a Catholic kindergarten in a village ten minutes away from Kastel improved our financial situation as well.

We celebrated our achievements with tea and pastries on our veranda. As we were sitting together, I began to adapt myself to the new challenges that awaited me at grammar school. Even though I believed that my educational achievements were good, a strange feeling told me that I might have to make difficult decisions in the new school that would deeply affect my identity.

III. Kastel

September 1997-August 2003

"The way to justice requires courage"

Monday, September 8, 1997

I transferred to Weinbergschule (WBS), a flat-roofed concrete building. WBS included a Hauptschule, a Realschule, and a grammar school. Mamun and Alim attended the Realschule. I was glad I could see them on the school grounds during the breaks. Furthermore, Marcus and I attended the same class at the grammar school. We were looking forward to spending the next six years together. *We had become best friends.*

On our first school day, we were sitting side by side in our new classroom when our new class teacher, *Mr. Siegert,* asked us to introduce ourselves. Marcus began. I followed, noticing that I stood out. Out of 31 students, I was the only boy with black hair, brown eyes, and relatively brown skin. When Mr. Siegert asked only me where I was "originally from," everyone, except Marcus, scrutinized me from head to toe. I felt odd and quickly explained my parents' nationalities. Next, Mr. Siegert asked the same question only to the three girls that had black hair. Their parents were born in Mexico, Italy, and Turkey. Sitting in the classroom and experiencing how different physical appearances were put on the spot, my fear of possible rejection flared up again. Moreover, I even saw the possibility that *my skills could be linked with my different heritage. And if I did not perform well, I could easily be downgraded to Realschule.* I felt called on to prove to myself and to the others that I rightly belonged to grammar school.

Saturday, December 6, 1997

Despite my initial fears of failing at grammar school, I quickly befriended many classmates. Next to working together in the classrooms, we played soccer or basketball together almost every break. We also met in our free time more and more often, and usually, we had great fun.

Marcus's 11th birthday was a strange exception to our happy being together, however. He invited five boys from our class to celebrate his birthday in a thermal bath. Shortly after we had entered the changing room, everyone began to take off his clothes—completely. I was taken by surprise, wondering what was happening. When Marcus's father approached me with his uncircumcised penis, he said, "Junis, take off your clothes. We don't want to wait for you." I looked at him, baffled. I had never seen any of my family naked. It was considered very obscene. To make things worse, I noticed that I was the only one who was circumcised. I remembered how my classmates had already made fun of circumcision when we had talked about Judaism in religious instruction. "Why don't you take off your pants? Don't be shy!" *Finn* said. *Martin, Stephen, Marek, Christopher,* and Marcus laughed. I felt shown up, but there seemed to be no way out. Reluctantly, I turned my back on them, opened the locker door, stepped forward, so no one could see my penis, and pulled down my pants. They saw my naked bottom, which felt embarrassing enough. *My father would never have expected this of me! He would have even reprimanded me for it.* I felt out of place. "What are you hiding?" Stephen asked. I did not reply and turned red in the face while my classmates laughed again. Hastily, I put on my swimming trunks, closed the locker, and followed them. I felt ashamed of my strange body, ashamed of my strange shyness, ashamed of going against a behavior I had learned from my family.

Thursday, October 29, 1998

After attending WBS for more than a year, I thought I was doing well. My grades were good, and I had made many friends in class. The longer we knew each other, the more I learned that there was no good reason to be ashamed of myself even though I still avoided being naked in front of others. To-show-or-not-to-show-your-penis was not a meaningful everyday problem though, I learned. *My classmates appreciated who I was and vice versa.* We enjoyed being together, laughing, talking, and playing.

Moreover, I often met my former classmates from Pestalozzi Schule during the breaks. Hakim usually hung around with his new classmates at the cafeteria. We always shook hands and exchanged some words. Nasir and Ricardo's classroom was located in the same corridor as my classroom. We met and talked to each other several times a day.

Over our first school year, however, Nasir and Ricardo's classmates more and more often called my classmates names. It irritated me. I had not understood why they tried to provoke us until one day. "You fucking nerds. Get out of our ways, bitches!" they shouted at us. They spared me from verbal insults, but their looks expressed a similar contempt. When I approached Nasir and Ricardo, reaching out my hand and trying to talk with them to understand their classmates, they pulled back. I felt put down and yet responsible for their behavior. *Did they think I betrayed them, going to grammar school? Or did they think they were cooler, better than us?* Perplexed, disappointed, and sad, I walked to my classroom. *Were we not friends?*

While facing an unexpected breach with some former classmates, my new friendships in my new class grew stronger. *Helena* wrote in my friendship book, "Stay as funny as you are and keep dancing like MJ[37]! I like you completely, my dear." Everyone wrote in it, "I wish we could stay friends forever." I wished and hoped the same.

Friday, January 15, 1999

When I came home from school, my father handed me a letter. He looked at me, distressed, and said, "A letter from the lawyers of the Frankfurt higher regional court." I was

---

[37] born Michael Joseph Jackson (08/29/1958 - 06/25/2009), American singer, songwriter, dancer, and philanthropist, one of the most popular entertainers in the world

alarmed. *Why would they write to us?* I sat down and read the letter.

> Our clients wish, certainly more than you do, that the renovation work in your house ends one day. The noise has stressed our clients' neighborly tolerance more than is acceptable.
>
> The town council has informed us that you are allegedly interested in a good neighborly relationship. This is easily achieved if you adhere to the minimal requirement of social behavior, taken as self-evident by every man in this country:
>
> 1. Adhere to the quiet periods.
> 2. Inform your neighbors in advance of any noise-intense work, so they can avoid this time by running errands.
>
> Our clients' health is already damaged because of your behavior. This does not necessarily add to a good neighborly relationship. Our clients informed me that you have been the chairman of the Kasteler "Council of Foreigners" since 1997 and that you advise foreigners to adjust to local customs as far as possible. Apparently, this recommendation ends at your front door as you act unreasonably ruthless.

> In the interest of all parties, we ask you to show
> the little thoughtfulness that our clients expect.
> Since you ask our clients to tolerate the work, it
> would be only just if you paid consideration to
> their wish as well. If you lack this minimal social
> behavior, we will, unfortunately, advise our clients to sue you. We hope that this, as it is common
> with halfway civilized people, is not necessary.

I felt disgraced. *Halfway civilized? What a humiliating language!* I placed the letter on the table and looked at my father with a serious face, "What are we going to do now?"

"We'll wait until your mother comes. We'll make a plan together."

Shortly after, she came home from kindergarten. He gave her the letter. After she had read it, she told him, visibly upset, "We go to a lawyer right now!"

In the late evening, they returned with a copy of a letter written by a lawyer. I read it, slowly and attentively.

> It is correct that my clients hired construction
> companies to renovate the house in Paul-Ehrlich-
> Straße 4. However, the structural alterations
> were conducted in regular working times. Also, a
> violation against the township law of quiet hours
> did not occur since such a law does not exist in the

first place. We are ready to receive a copy of this township law from you if it exists.

Further, a violation of the noise-protection-regulations of Hesse did not occur. It is correct that nights (8 p.m. - 7 a.m.), midday quiet hours (1 p.m. - 3 p.m.), and holidays are protected from noise. This generally affects private households. Yet, § 3 of the law protection regulations says that services of registered firms are excluded. If the rest periods had been violated, it was not done by my clients but by the workers of registered firms, which are excluded from the noise protection regulations.

With regard to your other arguments, it has to be noted that they do not serve an objective dispute. This especially applies to the note that my client is active in the "Council of Foreigners." This note has no reasonable justification and shall apparently only serve as cheap propaganda. At this juncture, I may note that any further arguments in that direction will be prosecuted as libel.

For the reason of completeness, it has to be noted that your clients gave you incorrect information. Over the years, my clients have tried to build a neighborly relationship. Yet, all their greetings have been ignored in the last six years. No conversation could be held with your clients, who told the town council that they do not want to talk with my clients. When your clients telephone, they call my clients "anti-social, uncivilized foreigners who should go back where they came from" and hang up. When our clients meet on the street, your clients switch to the other side of the street with ostentation. Whether this is civilized behavior, shall not be discussed here.

My clients will, like in the past, adhere to the quiet hours. They are also interested in improving the social contact with your clients. Your client, however, should wish this as well. Last but not least, it shall be noted that, despite an eight-year long neighborly relationship, your clients do not know how to spell my clients' last name correctly.

I put down the letter and looked at my parents, relieved that they asserted through official channels our correct behavior toward the given rules and our willingness to restore a neighborly relationship. I even felt hopeful. *Even if our neighbors were not interested in a good relationship, the German authorities could at least find my family not guilty if we had to go to court.*

Saturday, February 6, 1999

A few weeks after our lawyer had sent out the letter, carnival season started. I was looking forward to having a fun and good time in contrast to the burdensome conflict with our neighbors.

By 1999, my siblings had joined the Kasteler band as well. We opened the first of what would be four carnival sessions in the Goldbachhalle[38] at 8 p.m. After the traditional three beats of our drums, our march through the rows began. The gymnasium was packed with hundreds of people. Some started to scream as if they were at an open-air concert. Even the elders got up and excitedly clapped their hands. Adrenaline shot through my veins. Soon, my heartbeat outran the beat of our forceful drums. We positioned ourselves on the stage and raised our wind instruments. I was standing in the front row, under the hot spotlight, when we began to play. Performing with the Kasteler band and captivating the people felt great.

After our performance, we got drinks and sandwiches free backstage. With more than 30 active members, our band was the largest club of the Kasteler Karneval Klub. We were thus granted permission to spend the time between our two performances in the smaller adjoining gymnasium.

During carnival, there were no constrictions. I liked that freedom. My parents let me stay out as long as I wanted. After our second performance at 10:30 p.m., most band members gathered on the stage in the adjoining gymnasium. We arranged tables and drinks to spend the rest of the night together, snacking, drinking, laughing, and playing table games. No one told us to be quiet. We could just be ourselves and enjoy

---

38   name of a Kasteler gymnasium

our time together. I had also brought my CD-player. When I put on "Top of the Pops"[39], many started to dance and sing. I felt warmly attached to every single person. At midnight, all the young children were driven home, while I was allowed to stay. Piero and I got drunk for the first time. One beer, one Jägermeister, one tequila, and cola for a change. Mamun and Alim drank as well while all the elders checked that we teenagers did not drink too much. I loved them all—*happy, uncomplicated, and kind people.*

At 3:30 a.m., Mamun, Alim, and I started to amble home. When we reached the railway station, a skinhead started to harass us. I was probably too drunk to notice, but Mamun did. "Hurry up, Junis!" he told me and grabbed my hand. Fortunately, we were almost home.

Saturday, February 13, 1999

We were watching the news around noon, "The 28-year-old Algerian Asylum seeker Farid Giendoul was persecuted to death in Guben, Brandenburg. He was attacked by three neo-Nazis at night and somehow managed to run away. While the chase continued, he desperately broke in a glass door and cut an artery in his leg. He bled to death while the neo-Nazis watched him dying."

We looked at each other, shocked by another hate-crime. *The poor man!* Suddenly, the other night when we were

---

39 collection of popular current chart songs across all genres

persecuted flashed up in my mind. *We just made it home in the nick of time.* Fear caught up with me again.

Friday, Mai 21, 1999

Despite the ongoing conflict with our neighbors, we took further steps to make our house a home.

We pulled down all the rotten carpets from our rooms as well as the dissolving linoleum from our hallway. It was a tough job. Several layers of carpets and linoleum had been glued on each other. We were coughing nonstop even though we wore respirators. Still, it felt good to see that we were able to make room for new, clean, and cozy interior furnishings.

Thursday, May 27, 1999

A company laid beige tiles in our house. Afraid we could again receive complaints from our neighbors, my parents asked the tilers to work as quietly as possible. The two men laughed, "There's nothing wrong in what we are doing here. We have a job to do. We don't care about your neighbor's special requests. You shouldn't either." *They were absolutely right,* I thought and wished my parents were more self-confident.

Beginning of January 2000

Nine years after the war, my family was finally reunited. Manal came to Germany with her children because her son had almost died from diarrhea. The ongoing UN sanctions were still silently killing people in Iraq in high numbers. Manal and her children moved into our house for the time being, and I was glad to be with them.

We all got along well. My siblings and I played with *Asis,* my 4-year-old nephew, and *Amal,* my 2-year-old niece, every day after we came home from school. We would put them in their buggies and race on bicycle lanes to the next playground while they would laugh themselves to tears.

Despite the joy we shared, my family had new problems to solve. Our income was not sufficient to feed nine people and pay the bills. My mother repeatedly urged my father to quickly find a solution. But even though he took more double shifts, we still could not live in peace. Our neighbors sent us more letters, complaining that our house was "overcrowded" and that "civilized people would never share a small house like ours with nine people." *As if there were no other problems in the world.* I was sick of our neighbors' blind hate.

Tuesday, September 19, 2000

I found the Frankfurter Rundschau[40] (to which my father subscribed) on our kitchen table. I skimmed through it. "Right-wing violence claimed 93 deaths in Germany from 1990 to 2000," was one title. *What a shame!* I thought, and yet I was aware for the first time that the mainstream me-

---

40 German daily newspaper, based in Frankfurt am Main

dia revealed some numbers about that problem. I felt hopeful. *Widespread awareness could be the first step to tackle racism more systematically.*

Wednesday, November 1, 2000

After we had been harassed by our next-door neighbors for six years, we had to appear before the local court of Frankfurt to testify in the case "Schmidt vs. Sultan." We were sued by our neighbors for noise disturbances. We countersued them for:

1. Putting up a 6-feet-high wooden wall at the property border without informing us and without our agreement
2. Bullying us in different ways, such as:
    a) Beating against the living room wall, chopping wood, hammering against the pipe in the basement, throwing around wooden objects in the veranda, playing loud marching songs and Heimatlieder on Saturday mornings before 7 a.m.
    b) Glaring at all family members and visitors through the kitchen window (or other windows) round the clock
    c) Frequently sending us insulting letters with lists about alleged violations against the noise regulations

d) Trying to intimidate us through insulting telephone calls and by talking to third parties

I felt exceptionally nervous. Never had I seen a courtroom from the inside until I was sitting in one, as a 14-year-old defendant. *How would the judge decide?*

When the judge entered the hall, everyone became silent. He presented our case. Next, he asked my parents to come to the front to testify on part 1 and 2 a) of the lawsuit.

After their testimony, he called me to testify on part 2 b). When I sat down in front of him, I briefly turned around to my parents. They looked at me, expectant. I was worried I might say something that would get us into trouble. *Yet, being silent was no option either,* I knew. *It would definitely not help my family.* I summoned my courage and took a deep breath.

I said, "When we bring out the garbage, when we collect the mail, when someone rings the bell, the curtains in our neighbors' kitchen are moved aside and our neighbors glare at the person in our front garden. When we come home from school, they glare at us from behind their kitchen window. When we play in our backyard, they lower their roller blinds and observe us through a small gap. When we enter our veranda at night, they follow immediately and switch on the light in their veranda. They observe every step we make."

The judge took some notes before he looked at me with a stern face. "Can you comment on the noise disturbances?" he asked.

I looked at him, baffled and wondering. *I was not a criminal. Was I?*

Our neighbors began to laugh.

"Be quiet! Otherwise, you will get a warning," he shouted at them.

He seemed to want to solve the case quickly and in fair terms. Half-intimidated, half-confident, I continued to speak, "I don't have the chance to make noteworthy noise. When I listen to music at medium volume, our neighbors call immediately. They call me "antisocial" and request me to stop making noise. Next, they send insulting letters. In 2000, they also called the police, who sometimes appeared, in vain. My parents always urge me to stay quiet. In the rest periods, they don't even allow me to listen to music at room volume. I have to listen to music with earphones. When I move furniture, they come and tell me to stop it immediately, even outside the rest periods. They have also urged me to inform my neighbors about my birthday party. When I called them, they hung up the phone right away."

I turned around and looked at my neighbors—suddenly feeling freed. Finally, I spoke up against their tormenting injustices. Finally, I was heard after all those years of being persecuted in my own house, of having to stay silent or justify every tone, of being denied the right and the chance to develop myself without constraints, threats, and fear.

The judge asked me to sit down.

I sat next to my father, who grabbed my hand.

"Good job, Junis," he whispered.

"Thank you. I gave my best," I replied and began to reflect. *The way to justice requires courage. It can be long and painful, but it's inevitable for a dignified life.*

Sunday, December 24, 2000

A few weeks after the stressful court experience, Christmas season started. Since Manal found a small apartment for low-income families in Kastel, we decided to stay and not celebrate Christmas in Amtal as in the previous years. We celebrated at Paul-Ehrlich-Straße 4. Oma Erika, Nour, and her family came as well. I was happy about our get-together.

Delighted, I videotaped our warm, festive living room. White pillar candles were shining on our brown marble window sill. Our windows were decorated with the colored paper stars, flying angels, and running deer. Red pillar candles were shining on our white coffee table between plates with ambrosial almond cookies and kletsha while "Stille Nacht," a classic German Christmas song, lightly filled the room with a harmonious chorus.

The music came from the speakers of our new 32-inch silver television that had cost 1,800 DM. After we had spent several years struggling economically, I was still aware of the costs of items. In fact, our budget was still tight because we had spent a lot of money on renovating our house. Nevertheless, my mother wanted to surprise us with a new television a few days before Christmas, and she did. Our house was finally completely updated after nine years of hard work.

Rahila was standing next to our shiny Christmas tree. Red and golden globes were twinkling from the branches. She waved with both hands at the camera, smiling. Suddenly, Sophia jumped into the picture and threw kisses to Rahila. All three of us laughed full-heartedly.

My family gathered in the living room. Christmas was still one of the best times of the year for me, *a time of togetherness, kindness, and joy.*

Still, this Christmas was different. Ammu Amir had come to Germany and joined our Christmas feast for the first time. Silent and strained, he was sitting on our couch. He was unable to speak and understand German. My father tried to accommodate him. He brought him fruits from our kitchen. "People in Iraq usually sit together at night and eat fruits," he spoke into the camera. I noticed, somewhat startled, how much our family evenings in Iraq had passed out of my mind. When I videotaped Asis, Asis jumped up from the couch with a big smile, "I love Christmas. I want to be a snowman. I want to swim in snow." From the corner of my eye, I saw Ammu Amir staring at him with lowered eyebrows. My father tried to distract him from Asis's enthusiasm by starting a conversation in Arabic while I wondered what Ammu Amir was thinking about us. *Stupid Christmas? Stupid Europeans? Maybe even stupid family?*

For a second, I videotaped Ammu Amir, who still looked like Saddam Hussein with his mustache and short, wiry hair combed to the back. Within this second, Ammu Amir glared at me.

"Don't videotape him! They don't like it in Iraq," my father told me.

I switched off the camera. Ammu Amir's behavior appeared strange to me. "Why?" I asked, perplexed and remembering how we used to take pictures in Iraq all the time.

"Taking pictures of living creatures is not forbidden in the Quran, but some people advise against it to avoid adoring anyone or anything else but Allah," he said.

Really? I felt at a loss for the first time on Christmas.

After everyone had eaten, Sophia lit two sparklers in front of our tree. Everyone, except Ammu Amir and my father, clapped their hands. "The small ones will now hand out the presents," Sophia said in a sweet voice. We thanked and hugged each other for the presents. Ammu Amir received some presents as well. He looked at them suspiciously and asked my father what the presents were about. To my surprise, my father acted as if Christmas was strange to him as well. When he received his presents, he said, "For me? Presents? What for?" His behavior made me wonder. *Did he intend to comfort Ammu Amir, who felt odd celebrating a Christian feast as a Muslim? Or did he also not want to celebrate Christmas as a Muslim anymore? Why then did he celebrate Christmas with us in Iraq? Was he not concerned about it because our surroundings were predominantly Muslim in Iraq? Did he need to reaffirm his identity in Christian dominant Germany? Or was he simply becoming more religious now that he grew old and needed something familiar to hold on?*

Thursday, February 22, 2001

For whatever reasons, my father was becoming more religious. A few days after Christmas, he announced during teatime that he would go to Mecca and do the pilgrimage. He said it meant a lot to him and that he wanted to go before he would become too old and weak. He was 61 years old. My mother complained that the trip would be too expensive, but he had already booked it. So, he went to Mecca.

One afternoon in February, we received a postcard from Mecca. The picture showed thousands of Muslims in white garments encircling the Kaaba[41]. On the backside, my father wrote, "Blessings to you from God. Maybe I shall reach you before this card does. I challenge you to try to find me in the crowd of this picture. I love you."

Mid-March 2001

My father's trip to Mecca brought back many questions to my mind that I had often asked myself throughout the years. *What was Islam? Who was I? Was I a Muslim, too?* Since I had read a short text about Islam in religious education at school, I only vaguely

---

41 building at the center of Islam's most sacred mosque, al-masjid al-harām, in Mecca, al-Hejaz, Saudi Arabia

knew that going to Mecca was one of the five pillars of Islam. I was looking forward to finally learning more about Islam from my father even though I also felt a bit uneasy about his return. *Would he come back as a different person? With strict religious beliefs and practices? If so, would we be affected? If yes, how?*

The bell rang in the afternoon. He was wearing a full, white beard—for the first time. In Iraq, only old or religious people wore this beard. He was both now, I noticed, strangely surprised. We smiled and hugged each other for an unusually long moment. I was glad to see him again despite my unspoken concerns. He, on the other hand, seemed completely relaxed.

At a leisurely pace, he walked to our living room. He opened his suitcase and handed out a photo to everyone. In the photo, he was standing on a white marble floor, wearing a white cloth. His look into the camera was determined. It reminded me of his inner strength. *He had overcome many difficulties after "Operation Desert Storm."* I felt proud of him.

Next, he handed out a golden necklace to everyone. I looked at it, carefully. It held a pendant that looked like a scroll. "Allah" was engraved on one side, "Muhammad" on the other. Those were the few words, next to my name, I had learned from him in Arabic years ago. Feeling honored, I put the necklace on. We smiled at each other again.

"There's something else," he said. "You've asked me many times, and I always tried to dissuade you. But if you still want to box, I'll find a club for you."

I looked at him with large eyes, almost in disbelief.

Shortly, my mother left the room.

I was perplexed. *Was she upset because I wore the necklace or because I would start boxing?*

After a little while, she returned with a small, red box in her hand.

"This is the Cross my father used to wear. It's for you," she told me.

I was speechless. Her father had died from cancer in 1989. From among all her children, she picked me to wear his Cross. I had no idea why, but I felt awfully honored and yet ashamed since my siblings looked at me with empty hands.

"Just take it," she said.

I hugged her and put the Cross on as well.

From that day on, I carried two pendants that represented my father's and my mother's religion, and I felt good about cherishing both of their religions.

Wednesday, March 21, 2001

After school, my father handed me a letter with a contented smile on his face. "Read this! It's by the local district court of Frankfurt," he said. I began to read.

> In the name of the people: In the lawsuit: Mr. and Ms. Schmidt (claimants) and Mr. and Ms. Sultan (defendants) the court of Frankfurt adjudged to dismiss the case. The lawsuit's cost will be carried to 7/10

```
by the claimant and 3/10 by the accused. Grounds:
The claims are without merit. The accused are own-
ers of the property in Paul-Ehrlich-Straße 4 and
have the right to renovate their property as
they like. No third party can request them to
reduce the renovation to a minimum as long as it
does not violate public regulations.
```

I smiled and hugged him, thankful that justice was finally served. *Our years-long struggles had come to a happy ending. What could come in our way now?*

Friday, June 29, 2001

My family and I went on a two-week vacation in Denia, Spain. Our destination was located at the slope of the Montgo, a mountain that defined the skyline with its rocky cliffs and sleeplike formations.

We entered our vacation house on a pebble stone driveway. As we got out of our Toyota Previa, our new family van that we had bought the previous year, I spotted something behind some rose bushes that made me cheer and shout, "Our own swimming pool?!" "Surprise!" my parents said, "The long journey was not in vain, kids." My siblings and I ran to the pool and marveled at the sight. Three white lounge chairs were positioned next to the pool. A stone grill was close by. A lowered terrace led to a wooden, dark brown front door. The house's name was affixed on it in blue letters, "Eleonora." *It sounded so harmonic and peaceful.*

Joyful, we followed my parents into the one-story house, which turned out to bigger on the inside than we had expected. The spacious living room contained three couches that pointed toward a fireplace and a large television. The ceiling was extra high, about 15 feet. To our left, we spotted an open kitchen, which contained a refrigerator, a boiler, and all kinds of house appliances. "We also have three bedrooms and two bathrooms," my parents announced. I was impressed by the size and the interior furnishing of our vacation house.

It was about 9:30 p.m., two hours after we had arrived, unloaded the car, and put everything in the closets, when Sophia, Alim, and I jumped in our swimming pool. Mamun videotaped us with a bag in his hand that contained flippers, snorkels, and diving masks. Smiling, he threw the bag in the water. We swam after it and started tickling each other, so that no one was able to get to the bag. In the background, my CD-player was playing *Phil Collins's*[42] "Another Day in Paradise." *What a dream vacation!* It was still warm outside even though the sun had set down. No one complained about us having fun. I felt happy and at ease. My parents were sitting on the terrace. They drank tea and watched us amusedly.

---

[42] born 01/30/1950, English singer, songwriter, instrumentalist, record producer, and actor

Saturday, June 30, 2001

Next morning, I jumped rope on our terrace to stay fit. Jumping, I looked at the beauties that grew in our backyard: olive, lemon, and palm trees. When my father walked toward me, he said, wistful, "We've got the same trees in our garden in Yarmouk." His comment made me wonder. *When would he recover from the loss of Iraq? And who was meant by "we"?* Suddenly, reality caught up with me again. Even though Mosul, our gardens, our relatives and friends, and so much more was so far away from me, further than for my father, a small word like "we" reminded me of *the loss we all had to bear in some or the other way.*

Monday, July 9, 2001

We visited the castle of Denia, which housed an archaeological museum about the history of Denia and Spain. The part that discussed how Spain experienced a cultural and economic heyday during the Arab-Muslim era was particularly interesting for me. It informed me about a part of history that was largely neglected in school since our history lessons predominantly dealt with Germany, Europe, and North America. "Back then, Denia became the capital of a Taifa kingdom.[43] The word 'Denia' has Arabic roots and means 'low land,' " my father

---

43 independent Muslim-ruled principality, usually an emirate, formed in Al-Andalus (Moorish Iberia) after the final collapse of the Umayyad Caliphate of Córdoba in 1031

read out. I joined him reading through another panel and felt like learning something about my heritage. *I hardly knew anything about Arab-Muslim history.*

After we left the museum, we walked along the castle wall to look out over Denia. More and more ships entered the harbor as night drew near. Around 9 p.m., we watched the sunset. Its bright color looked like burning aluminum. We had never seen the sun in that intense color. We were awed.

After some silent minutes, my mother, looking at Denia, said to my father, "I've seen these gas-lamp-like street lights in another city yesterday, between Denia and Calpe. What was the name of that city again?

"Bin Isa," he said.

"You mean Benissa?"

"Bin Isa!" he said and touched her nude shoulders with his hands.

"Bin Isa?" she stared at the ground, skeptical, and walked away.

"And here we have a conflict again about whether one should pronounce Spanish words in Arabic or not," Alim said, annoyed.

"We've just read about Arabic influence in the museum. 'Bin' means 'son of' and 'Isa' is the name for 'Jesus' in the Quran," my father told us.

Taking a deep breath, I put my hands on the sandy castle wall. "Why do you guys have to argue about a name at this moment instead of enjoying our time? It's just about the name of a city," I said.

"It's not just a name of a city; it's about heritage! I want you to see that Arabs also have a rich, influential history. If your mother doesn't want to see that, I'm sorry for her," he said.

"But we've just seen that in the museum! Isn't that enough? Why do you create an ideological argument and kill our spirit of togetherness right now when we're on vacation together? We don't get the opportunity to enjoy ourselves every day," I said, sensing that *this was not the right time for ideological arguments, especially not for those destructive ones that aimed to undermine the value of another person's cultural background.*

Except for this argument at the Castle in Denia, we had a joyful and peaceful time together in Spain.

Tuesday, September 11, 2001, around 3 p.m.

I was eating rice with tomato-okra sauce at our kitchen table when the unexpected happened. My father was washing the dishes behind me. The radio was on. Suddenly, the radio announcer interrupted the music, "Attention! Breaking news—a plane accident just happened in Manhattan. One tower of the World Trade Center was damaged."

We went to the living room at once. He turned on the television and switched to CNN[44]. A picture of a smoky

---

44 Cable News Network, an American basic cable and satellite television news channel

tower was shown. "A plane just crashed into the tower," the reporter said. I was shocked. *The poor people inside the plane! The poor people inside the building!* "How can such an accident happen in New York?" I asked my father. He shrugged his shoulders. Shortly after, another plane flew into the second tower. I was horrified. *What is happening in the United States?* I asked myself, suspecting the worst. When another plane crashed into the Pentagon half an hour later, I knew that all this was no accident. *THIS was a new era of warfare.* I was scared!

WEDNESDAY, SEPTEMBER 12, 2001

Next morning, I had PE in the first two periods. We were waiting for Mr. Siegert in front of the gym. It was chilly outside. Summer had bowed out. Everyone was strangely silent and still, except for Finn, who approached me.

Finn was one of my close friends. We often met after school. Our classmates respected him. His father was the principal of a vocational school in Hofheim.

"Junis, what do you think? Who attacked the U.S.A.?" he asked.

"I've got no idea," I said.

He looked at me with large eyes, "My father said it was Saddam Hussein."

Baffled, I asked, "How can your father know if not even the U.S.A. does?"

"Because Saddam is a criminal. He and the Iraqis will get punished for it. And Osama bin Laden[45] and everyone who was involved, too. You'll see!" he told me with a raised finger.

I looked at him, perplexed. *How could he be so convinced without having any evidence and, on top, so craving for vengeance? And how could he treat me as if I was to blame as well?*

I looked around and faced judgmental eyes. *Did my classmates think the same?*

Their looks reminded me of the German chancellor *Gerhard Schröder,* who guaranteed unconditional solidarity with the U.S.A. and with the free and civilized world to fight the terrorists who stood behind the attacks and bring them to justice. Yet, I sensed that *Bush, Schröder, Finn, my classmates, and probably many other Germans confused justice with revenge.*

Before I could respond, however, Mr. Siegert came to open the gym. Everyone turned their back on me and followed him. I could not believe what was happening. *After all those years, they just left me standing alone without a word? Were we not friends?* Suddenly, I felt a piercing pain in my chest. I almost wanted to go home, but then Helena came back outside. "Junis, come in. They'll all calm down again," she said. We looked into each other's eyes. I hesitated, but then I followed her. My hope that she was right was stronger than my fear.

---

[45] founder of al-Qaida, the organization that claimed responsibility for the 9/11 attacks on the United States

Still, what followed felt completely surreal. My classmates and I did not speak with each other during our basketball game, as if we were playing on two separate teams: them against me and me against them. The silence between us felt agonizing.

After PE, we crossed the school grounds together, almost as usual if they had not quickly walked ahead of me without looking back once. I felt that our bond was broken. Distraught, I stopped at the cafeteria, where I, all of a sudden, found myself in the middle of a mass brawl—white against non-white Germans. This type of fighting had happened before but not at that magnitude. I stood rooted to the ground, aghast, while Marcus and some of my classmates fired their fists. Suddenly, a random guy came from the side and punched me in my kidneys. I turned around and knocked him down. When his friends saw me, I started to run to my classroom as fast as my legs could carry me. I was clearly outnumbered. *9/11 turned WBS into an open battlefield!*

Thursday, September 13, 2001

Our principal held a speech in the gym in front of the 800 students of WBS. He mourned the victims of 9/11 and also asked us "to stop the attacks on the foreign students, who are not to blame." Some students reacted promptly, shouting, "Ausländer raus!" ("Foreigners out of here!").

The principal's words were fruitless. I felt dismayed.

Gradually, I understood, *Group mentality often subdues individual awareness.* On top, such mass responses seemed to occur even more in times of modern media spreading fear through multiple channels day and night. I and many other "Middle Eastern" looking people were targeted because of our different appearance that the mainstream media, round the clock, put on a level with threat and terrorism. *School was no safe place for me anymore. Germany was no safe place for me once again. "The West" was no safe place for me after 9/11.*

END OF SEPTEMBER 2001

Sitting in the classroom and facing my new reality, I felt tormented by questions, lack of understanding, and anger. *How many moments had my classmates and I enjoyed together before 9/11? Were all those moments, all these years meaningless? How could our bonds vanish so easily?*

We barely approached each other now. Even though we had never talked about 9/11 again, I sensed that *who I was and which side I was on* remained a fundamental question for them.

One day, during our five-minute break, Marek came up to my table. He gave me a picture, which he had drawn during the lesson, and waited for a response.

"You observed my necklace well," I said.

"You carry a Quran pendant and a Cross. I've never seen that before. I wonder—do you feel more Muslim or Christian? I mean, are these religions even compatible at all?"

"Why shouldn't they?"

"Because they're so different and because I've never seen anyone who carried both."

"As regards the latter, you're probably right."

"But with which religion do you identify yourself more?"

"It's not *either or* for me. I pick what I value from *both* religions. Christianity and Islam have much in common and can be complementary in beautiful ways if you allow them to be," I said, noticing how many of my classmates observed me with ears up and wide eyes.

I felt stressed and began to ponder. *Did I really have to explain myself to people who had claimed to be my friends? Did Marek insist that I was a stranger after all? Or did he try to determine that I wasn't one? Why would he need to ask any of those questions when he had known me for years?* All I knew was that *I used to have a good relationship with my classmates, until 9/11!*

Monday, October 15, 2001:
First Diary Entry

I'm sitting at the white folding table in my room, in front of a blank paper. I'll start to write a diary now. Maybe it'll help me understand this life.

Today was my first school day after our two-week fall vacation. Marcus asked our class teacher if he could sit in the front row next to Finn. He was allowed to do so. When he removed his books from under our table, he told me he could focus better in the front row. I know the last row sometimes fooled around during the lessons and that it wasn't helpful to follow our teachers all the time, but I think there is more behind his decision.

After school, we always walked down Weinbergstraße together. It used to take us 20 minutes even though it's only 600 yards. We used to stroll and talk a lot. When we reached the Goldbachhallen, we often stood there another 15 minutes, chatting and laughing before we would go in different directions. Since 9/11, it feels like our walk has become an unpleasant obligation for both of us. We don't talk enthusiastically anymore. Instead, Marcus accelerates our walking speed. Sometimes, it feels like he is concerned about being seen with me. It hurts.

I don't understand Marcus's behavior. He is a Christian; I am not. So what? I don't believe in religious exclusivism. I was raised with two religions. Is it my fault that I'm related to Islam through my father? Is religion all that matters now? Then what about religious freedom? Even if I were a Muslim, Marcus wouldn't have the right to ostracize me. Is our constitution only a piece of paper? What about my human dignity? And what about human reason? Have I ever given him a reason to let religion come between us? I went to his confirmation when we were 13 years old. I ate pork and celebrated with his family. I appreciated him as he was—funny, sarcastic, and outgoing. We spent every season together. We played beach volleyball, and we threw girls into the swimming pool. We hung around with friends and drank beer from the gas station at night. We organized big house parties. We dreamed of a lifelong friendship as neighbors living next door ... How can our friendship suddenly be of no value?

SATURDAY, AUGUST 24, 2002: DIARY ENTRY

Two weeks ago, summer vacation ended. I've survived school so far. My classmates and I talk again, but I feel the cold distance between us. I feel without a friend in this world.

THURSDAY, SEPTEMBER 5, 2002: DIARY ENTRY

A lot of things will change because I want them to change, and they'll have to accept it. I'm no longer the 4-year-old boy who is incapable of speaking German. Today, I'm 16 years old, and I can hardly speak Arabic. It's a shame. How could I forget who I am and assimilate to this society? I French-kissed several girls "to have fun." I smoked and got wasted every weekend with so-called friends who let me down when things got rough. After 9/11, I started hanging out and doing shit with my friends from Hauptschule, mostly immigrants. Last weekend, we stole food from the supermarket and sprayed graffiti on the streets. I was rude, ignorant, and recently even criminal. I was everything but self-confident. I just followed along and tried to be like everyone else to get their acceptance without even knowing who I really was.

All this will stop today because I now know who I am. I AM JUNIS SULTAN! Does this sound like a German name? I am somewhat brown. Do I look like an "ethnic German"? I am circumcised. Is this required by Christianity? I was born to be a Muslim. THIS WAY I can believe in myself again after all the disappointments I've experienced and all the misdeeds I committed.

In this society, many people live misguidedly and don't think about the meaning of life. But I do criticize myself. I've lived mistakenly, and I want to live a meaning life.

What is a meaningful life? Many people blindly strive to attain material things and then die at some point. However, I want to create something meaningful, something I have dreamed of, something that hopefully stays for the benefit of other people. Oh, politicians and bankers, I don't merely want to attain material securities or increase my assets! I want to be the person who I want to be, Junis Sultan, the one who lives his dreams, the boxer, the son, the brother, the friend, someone who brings people together.

I'm not happy with the false and dysfunctional life I have lived. I have lacked something crucial that would give me inner strength on my journey to live a good life.

Since my classmates and I drifted apart, I have studied the Quran, and I found shelter, a sense of belonging, and guidance like never before, neither at home nor at school nor in friendships. Islam teaches me that we all belong to Allah's creation; that we have the right to life and the obligation to live in brotherhood; that we should be thankful and patient, and that we should trust Allah *that our lives are part of a divine, wonderful plan. Everything in my life happens for a good reason, I believe now, even if I do not see it now. I'm thankful to Allah for everything I've experienced. Alhamdulillah.*

It was about 6 p.m. My parents were sitting at the kitchen table, drinking their second cup of tea, when I positioned myself between them to declare my religious decision.

"I have to tell you something. From this day on, I'm a Muslim," I said.

"You, you what?" my mother said with wide eyes.

"I want to understand and speak Arabic. I want to study the Quran in its original language. I want to pray and live a good life. I thought you could support me."

She looked at my father, perplexed, "Say something!"

"He's free to choose his religion. If he needs support, I'll help him."

"Are you sure?" she asked me.

"Yes. I am a Muslim now."

"Why don't you first study Islam? Maybe you'll change your mind then," she said.

"I've read the Quran in German and many other books about Islam in the last few weeks. I'm not asking for permission. I just wanted to inform you," I said, sensing that she disregarded my decision but also hoping that she would accept it eventually. *Freedom of religion was my human right.* They told me so at school, and I believed in it. Without another word, I went upstairs to my room.

Friday, September 6, 2002

When I came home from school, I found my father sitting in front of the television, watching Al Jazeera[46] with a tense face. A map of Iraq was shown.

"The U.S.A. bombed an Iraqi air base near Baghdad. It's their preparation for another big war. The war against the axis of evil, as Bush claims," he said with contempt.

I was worried. I let him read the news-banner before I said, "I watched the German news this morning. They said the U.S. Congress had been informed that Saddam Hussein is close to developing a nuclear bomb and weapons of mass destruction (WMDs)."

"All lies and cheap propaganda[47] in favor of the U.S. economy and the Machiavellian[48] wish to get in Iraq and control the region," he said.

"I pray there'll not be another war," I said, distressed and pondering. "I just can't believe it. It's so irrational what the United States claims, and so many countries decry it."

He shrugged his shoulders. "If they want that war, they'll get it, even if it means lying to the entire world. They have the strongest army. They will not lose. They will go to Iraq and destroy everything, once again."

---

46 Arabic, literally "The Island," refers to the Arabian Peninsula, Doha-based broadcaster

47 David Miller. 2003. *TELL ME LIES: Propaganda and Media Distortion in the Attack on Iraq.* London: Pluto Press

48 Machiavellianism, employment of cunning and duplicity in statecraft or in general conduct, word comes from Italian Renaissance diplomat and writer Niccolò Machiavelli (1469-1527)

Really? I felt upset. After a moment of silent despair, I slowly went upstairs and grabbed my diary.

Diary entry

George W. Bush[49] and his partners from politics and economy think they can do whatever they want. But what about other people's right to life? Should people in Iraq live in poverty and die in war because they live under a weak and corrupt government of a country that produces a lot of oil? Where is justice in this world? How much is a human being worth in this dollar world? Is the war really about revenge and security? Until today, the U.S.A. has brought no solid proof that Saddam was responsible for 9/11 or that he has WMDs. If this war becomes a reality, I don't know where we are going. This war would be completely illegitimate!

Sunday, September 8, 2002: diary entry

My mother went to Amtal yesterday after she had quarreled with my father. She blamed him for watching the Arab news day and night and becoming more and more depressed. Even though what she noticed is right, I also understand his worries. It's not only

---

49 served as the 43rd President of the United States from 2001 to 2009

about politics. It's also about our relatives and friends in Iraq. Still, or maybe because of that, she doesn't want Iraq to become a topic of compassion in our house. She said Saddam and everyone who followed or tolerated him deserves punishment. I think there is more behind her behavior. After I had declared my faith, I stopped wearing the Cross even though I felt bad about taking it off since it had belonged to my grandfather. It just seems impossible to follow two religions in this torn world. She has not spoken with me since then. When I came home after school on Friday, she ran to the basement with tears in her eyes. She hid downstairs for hours. She doesn't want me to be a Muslim. Our separation hurts me deep inside. I feel sad and helpless. I love her. Of course, I want to have a relationship with my mother but also with myself. But how? How can I connect with her if she does not accept my personal freedom? I want to choose who I am.

I guess the only thing I can control is myself.

I wonder who else do I want to be and how do I get there? I want to be an educated person. I'll thus continue to study diligently. Also, I want to be a modest and healthy person. I'll therefore distance myself from consumerism. I don't need to buy costly brand-name clothes anymore. I'm thankful for everything I already have and for the basic things I can obtain. My nutrition will also get simpler: water, organic food, and no more junk food and drinks. I'll take care of my physical health. Finally yet importantly, I want to be a successful person. With respect to my dream of becoming a boxer, I'll apply a maximally efficient workout to perfect my boxing skills.

September 9, 2002: Diary Entry

I'm gradually becoming the person I want to be. I've worked out very hard in the last few months. I've become faster, stronger, and technically more advanced. Regularity, progressive intensity, rest periods, and the study of boxing fights have improved my boxing skills significantly. I can already spar with adults without difficulty.

Moreover, I've become one of the best students in my class as a result of applying most of my workout principles at school or at home when I study. I rarely have any leisure time. Instead, I have success now.

Mid-September 2002

One afternoon, my family and I were drinking tea in the kitchen. As usual, my mother took the floor. She spoke about her work and told us about a colleague who had a baby. Smiling, she raved about the baby's soft, light skin and blue eyes.

Out of the blue, she announced, "I want to adopt a German baby."

I was stunned. *Was she serious?* I looked at my father and my siblings, who slurped their tea, unimpressed. *Did they understand what she had just said?*

"You already have six children. Why would you adopt another child?" I asked.

Looking at her cup, she said, "Because I want to have someone who is like me."

"Are you saying that we're not like you?"

Mamun threw a stern look at me, but I did not care. I wanted to understand her.

"You're half-and-half, and I want a German child," she said, looking at me now.

I was perplexed. *What would a half-and-half human be?*

"Are we not all the same, just human beings?" I looked at her with raised eyebrows.

"You're different, and I want to have a German child," she repeated to herself.

My heart began to race. *Did she still believe that we were "different" because of "my father's inferior culture that was in us?"* I got up and spoke in a clear voice, "I don't have to sit here and listen to your degradations."

Everyone turned into stone, except my mother, who got up and raised her hand.

"Don't you ever dare touch me again! These times are over now. Touch me one more time, and you will never see me again!" I said.

She stared at me with large, surprised eyes, like everyone at the table, but I kept my strength of mind. Determined, I left.

Thursday, September 19, 2002:
diary entry

I was unhappy in the last few days. Even though I acted strong in front of my mother, I felt hurt when she claimed that we're so different from her. She's our mother! Who could be closer to us? Of course, we're different in some ways. Otherwise, we would be nothing but clones. Or does "culture" really come before blood?

At least, my physical performances progress. Today, PE was cancelled. When we were informed, my classmates went home, while I went to the athletic ground to run for one hour in the late-summer heat. The realization of my dreams requires constant and high efforts. I think I'm on the right track.

I also often talk with my father about Islam when we're alone. He answers most of my questions, but he's afraid to teach me Arabic. He said my mother "would not allow it," like in 1993 when she claimed that it would distract us from learning German. I wish it was not so unnecessarily complicated in my family.

Wednesday, October 16, 2002: diary entry

It's time to make a confession. I'm depressed, and I don't even know why. This incomprehensible feeling of despair assaults me time and again, and I feel helpless most of the time. Maybe I'm depressed because I expect too much from other people and from myself. Maybe I have unrealistic dreams. Yes, I'll take the driving test in two weeks. I'll also start working as a salesman in a men's boutique. Soon, I'll be able to buy a scooter. I'll be mobile then. Still, I know mobility is not what I'm looking for deep inside ... So what is my problem? Sometimes, I feel like I don't even know myself. Sometimes, I feel like I hate myself.

Sometimes, I feel like I could never fully connect with people. Sometimes, I think I could never be happy. Sometimes, I feel like this world is just torn and messed up. Do many people feel that way? Why do I ponder without an ending? Why do I feel so lonely and sad? Am I too self-centered?

Saturday, November 2, 2002: diary entry

I won my first fight by unanimous decision, alhamdulillah.

I pray five times a day. I have also ordered more books to learn more about the Prophet and the life of a Muslim. Islam gives me hope. It teaches me that I have intentionally been given life, that I am no mistake of my parents, and that Allah knows my life.

Monday, November 11, 2002

Even though Islam provided me with meaning and directions in some ways, it did not entirely ease my mind, my heart, and my soul in other ways. I was still looking for deep connections with other people. I wanted to know and understand them; and I wanted to be known and understood. I did not want to feel lonely.

Indeed, the relationship with my classmates recovered over the year. We gradually became closer again. Even though we had never verbalized our thoughts and feelings about what happened after 9/11, we, at some point, just started to spend some of our breaks together again. Usually, our breaks were trouble-free, until one day.

It was 11:25 a.m. when the school bell rang for the 15-minute break. Finn, Stephen, Martin, Marek, Marcus, and I left our classroom together. We walked around on the schoolyard until we stopped on the narrow lawn in front of the faculty room. Stephen was telling a joke when five students from Hauptschule approached us. I knew them through their older brothers. They greeted me from a distance. I greeted back.

Suddenly, Marcus said, "Look at these guys! One older than the other and all attending the sixth grade in Hauptschule. They're so desperately dumb."

Marek added straight away, "I bet they all have the same father. It's one guy who fucks his three or four wives and all his daughters and cousins. They tup women like rabbits, even their own children."

My heart began to race. I felt disgusted by their words.

Before I could intervene, however, Marcus shouted to them, "Look at me, Osama bin Laden! Alim! Mamun! Saddam! Amir! You understand what I say?"

"No, they can't. It's German," Marek said, smirking.

"What the hell is wrong with you guys?" I confronted Marcus and Marek.

"Eyyo, I gangster. I dangerous, blah blah blah. Just watch them. They're even dumber than they look. Watch that guy!

He's maybe just 13 years old and already has beard growth. I guess his ass is also covered with black hair," Marek said.

Everyone in our group began to laugh, except me.

I looked at the guy whom I used to think was my best friend. "Marcus! Seriously? You've known my family for years."

He turned his head toward Marek.

"So what?" Marek said, "Their older brothers fuck with us, too."

I looked at Marcus again, "You know the names of my brothers-in-law and of my brothers. You played with them for years. How can you call these guys by their names as if their names were an insult? Have you completely lost your common good sense?"

He raised his shoulders.

I felt completely betrayed. *He was even ready to verbally abuse my family.*

While the five boys came closer, I began to walk in their direction. The biggest one, half a head taller than me, shouted, "We didn't start it!"

"I know. Not this time," I said, stopping between both groups that seemed ready for another brawl. I looked one after the other in the eyes. "What the hell are you doing?" I shouted. "When will you finally stop?"

However, their faces showed only fear, hatred, and the willingness to destroy.

Upset, I walked back to my classroom, alone. I could not understand. *Why did they not at least get out of each other's way? Why did they look for an enemy to fight?*

WEDNESDAY, NOVEMBER 20, 2002: DIARY ENTRY

How could my classmates and I end up in such an ugly mess? Have we ever been true friends? How—if they enjoy bullying immigrants, people like my family and me? Am I also a despicable stranger in their eyes? Or do they really believe they can humiliate immigrants AND stay friends with me even though I am an immigrant as well? Do they really believe their behavior wouldn't affect me? Friends respect each other. They don't disgrace each other and each other's family. What happened is unacceptable.

My classmates and I barely talk with each other again. I only attend the lessons and afterward leave school. Our separation breaks my heart, but I don't know what else to do. I will not deny my identity and sell my dignity to be friends with them.

Whom can I trust these days? I feel almost hopeless. Ya Allah!

THURSDAY, NOVEMBER 28, 2002: DIARY ENTRY

Anyone who observed me in the last few weeks could say that I'm a weird, quiet boy who often walks around with a black eye. All of it would be true. I want to connect with people and just be myself. But who wants to love me as I am? I guess I have neither real friends nor a real family. Sometimes, Manal invites us to her apartment on Sundays. When I'm there, Ammu Amir often criticizes me in front of everyone. When I wear a T-shirt, he claims it's too revealing and allegedly haram. When I listen to music on my MP3-player, he claims that music seduces the senses and is thus allegedly haram. Even meeting, not to mention being friends with non-Muslims, is not okay for him. He abuses Islam with wrong or manipulative interpretations to pseudo-justify his total-control-over-everyone-agenda, while I'm tired of defending myself. My family doesn't defend me either. They care more about themselves.

According to Ammu Serhat, I'm basically blameworthy as well. He often speaks to me in Arabic and then laughs at me because I can't understand him. When we're in private, he tells me that I'm a shame to my family and to myself because I forgot Arabic. Does he believe that putting me down makes me a better Arabic speaker? Why does he not teach me Arabic if he's so great? Instead, he calls my bluff in front of everyone. He says I forgot where I come from. He doesn't know anything. Only Allah knows. Only Allah—and no one else—can judge me. Still, I wish I could just have one person who knows and understands me.

Thursday, December 26, 2002: diary entry

Piero and I have become close again. He attends Hauptschule at WBS. One day, I met him at the cafeteria. We began to talk about our good old time at the Kasteler band. I had left the band when I started boxing since I decided to focus on my dream and put in all the work to become a successful boxer. Anyway, we now *spend most of our breaks together. We also call each other almost every other day to meet up. We cruise around on my scooter and go to sports bars or to the cinema. We enjoy our time together. We always have something to laugh about. It feels good to be with Piero. I am thankful for knowing him.*

Saturday, January 18, 2003

I went to Piero's at 10:30 p.m. We were sitting on his sofa bed, sharing a bowl of chips and watching the 2002 movie version of Spider-Man when my cell phone rang.

Mamun spoke in a hurry, "Maybe no one will be at home when you come. We'll drive to the hospital now. Sophia just came home, drunk, screaming, lashing around. The ambulance said she had alcohol poisoning. Don't come, we're already leaving!"

Piero and I looked at each other. He saw it in my eyes.

"What happened?" he asked in a serious voice.

"I think someone got Sophia drunk," I paused. "She's not that stupid. She was in the youth club tonight. I'm gonna find out what happened," I said.

Piero got up right away. We raced to the youth club to find out that the police had already sent everyone home. So, I drove Piero back home as well and went to Paul-Ehrlich-Straße.

I was sitting on the stairs in our hallway, waiting, when someone put a key in the front door lock from the outside. My father and Mamun entered the hallway. They stopped next to me. Their faces were full of fear and disgust. My father turned around and stared at the front door. "We were watching Spider-Man when the bell rang. A mother of someone called Miriam laid your sister like a dead person in front of our door, right there," he paused. "She was fidgeting with her hands. She shouted, 'Miriam bad! Bad boys! Wanted to hurt me. You are angels.' "

I was scared. *What did they do to my sister? Who was Miriam? Who were these boys?* My relationship with Sophia was not very close. While I rejected mainstream society after 9/11, Sophia tried to be a part of it. Yet, I knew I would never allow anyone to hurt her.

"Baba, I will find out what happened," I said.

Monday, January 20, 2003

Piero and I walked around on the school grounds during the break and asked around about what had happened at the party the other night. We were told two guys got her drunk with Bacardi-Cola. We were also given their names: *Dennis* and *Patrick*. Shortly after we received that information, the break bell rang. We went back to our classrooms.

During my math course, I was called out by the principal, "Junis Sultan, Junis Sultan, to the principal's office, now!" Everyone in my class looked at me with big eyes, but I did not care about their judgment anymore. I left the classroom and went down to the first floor.

The principal was standing in front of her office. With a stern face, she said, "Come in. Sit down." Two police officers were already sitting at her long table. I was alarmed by their presence.

She began to speak, "We know what happened with your sister, and we're sorry. But it's not your business to do justice. Germany is a nation of law and order. We have a system of legislative, executive, and judicial power. I'm sure you've heard about it in class. It may be different from where you come from, but it's like that here."

"I know the German system," I said, unimpressed.

"We also know about your activities as a boxer from the newspapers," she continued. "If you hurt anyone, you'll be charged with grievous bodily harm because your hands count as a weapon. You'll lose your boxing license and flunk out from school. To be clear, I'll make sure you get the harshest punishment possible if anyone gets hurt. You understand?"

I looked at her, puzzled. *Did she call me in over rumors that I would take revenge? Or was she convinced that I'd respond in a violent way because of my heritage?*

"The officers will explain the consequences for you in Germany," she said.

While they started talking, I briefly looked outside the window. Immediately and involuntarily, I recalled the incident with the six graders of Hauptschule. I was lost in a flashback.

Suddenly, I heard one officer asking if I had questions.

I said, "No."

Everyone got up.

She asked if I would leave the boys alone.

"I can't guarantee anything," I said and left.

Thursday, January 30, 2003

During another lesson, I was called out again, "Junis Sultan, Junis Sultan to the pedagogical director, now!" I went down to the first floor and knocked at his open door. Mr. Siegert got up. He was my former class teacher and the teacher I respected most since he was strict but fair to everyone. He shook my hand. We sat down.

He sincerely looked into my eyes. "Junis, I'm so sorry for your sister, for you, and for your family."

"Can you imagine what such a thing means to a family like mine?" I asked.

"I think I can," he paused. "But don't do anything that gets you into trouble now. Please. Don't! Do it for me, for your family, for you, for your dream of boxing."

I suddenly felt as if the world was lying on my chest. I had difficulties breathing, but he waited—looking at me. I spoke in a shaky voice, "So what about justice? The law cares neither about my sister nor about my family. It doesn't care about how much we are mortified. These boys are teenagers. They'll not be punished. Only my sister, my family and I will, and nobody cares."

"Junis, I do. I will help you. But don't confuse justice with revenge! Don't!" he said.

I looked at him, pondering, and yet already sensing that he was right. *Beating up these boys wouldn't undo the injustice that had happened to Sophia. It would only add more violence and destruction to this world. And if I truly wanted it to be a better place, I had to resist—even if my anger wanted revenge.* Tears rolled down my cheeks. *I had to accept what had happened.* I nodded and said, "Okay."

He came to the front and put his hand on my shoulder, "Junis, I am here for you."

I got up and thanked him with a handshake before I slowly walked back to my classroom.

After the lesson, Marcus waited in front of our classroom. He was standing next to the orange lockers when I came outside. "Junis, I need to speak with you," he said.

"Go ahead," I said even though I was not in the mood for speaking, particularly not with Marcus, since I still had difficulties accepting the injustice my family had to overcome.

"I know what happened to your sister," he paused. "If I can help you, let me know."

"You want to help me?" I paused and looked him in the eyes. "The guys that got her drunk are your new friends. I don't need any help from a neo-Nazi like you."

"Do you know what you're saying? I'm no neo-Nazi!" he said with a raised eyebrow.

"You are. You just don't know. You think you can humiliate and beat up people who don't look, talk, and behave like you! I don't need your help."

"You've changed," he stepped back. "I drink, smoke, and do shit, and you used to do that with me as well, but you're not the same person anymore."

"Right. And now what?"

"I guess our friendship is over now."

"Yes, and not only as of today. You crossed the line last November," I said.

He gulped, turned around, and walked away. I looked behind him until he disappeared behind the lockers. I felt miserable, knowing that I absolutely lost my first friend in Germany.

Friday, February 14, 2003: diary entry

The day of lovers? Sure. My parents are making my life even harder than it is at the moment. They don't stop fighting. Day and night, they quarrel over whether "the" German culture is to blame for what had happened with Sophia, whether "the" Muslim upbringing would have prevented it, whether "the" Muslim way of life is inferior anyway. Blah blah blah.

At least, I have Piero. I need to get out of here.

Saturday, March 8, 2003, around 11 p.m.

Piero, Salvatore, and I were walking on the sidewalk of Bahnhofstraße. We were about 200 yards away from Paul-Ehrlich-Straße when a patrol car rapidly pulled up and stopped us.

"Put your hands on the wall! Spread your legs!" the officer shouted.

"What's the point of that? We didn't commit any crime," I said.

"Shut up!" he said. "We're looking for Mediterranean looking guys who just robbed and beat up a person at the railway station."

"Shit," I said, looking at ourselves. I was wearing a hoody under a black leather jacket. *Wrong look, wrong place, wrong time.*

He patted us down. His colleague, standing close by, kept a wary eye on us while her hand was on her pistol. He first looked for my cell phone, then for Piero's. "Boom," he suddenly said. "The cell phone we're looking for." His colleague called reinforcement.

Even though Salvatore did not understand German, he understood what was going on. "Porca puttana," he cursed. The police officer pushed him against the wall, "Shut up!" *We were in trouble,* I sensed.

Shortly after, another patrol car came from the railway station. We were standing with our hands on the wall while flashing blue light lit up the street. I briefly looked over my shoulder when Marcus and two more officers got out of the other patrol car.

"We got them," the officer said to Marcus, showing him Piero's red Nokia 7210. "Did these guys rob you and beat you up?" the officer asked him.

Marcus eyed my suspiciously before he said, "No."

"Check the contacts on the phone! It's my cell phone," Piero said to Marcus.

"I told you to shut the fuck up!" the officer shouted at us. "Last warning, boys. One more word and we will take you to our police station and have a real fun night."

They checked the contact list and made a call to the police station while dozens of roller blinds were raised. My neighborhood was watching the show. I felt disgraced.

Eventually, Marcus got back in the patrol car.

"Lucky you!" the officer said to us before he got into the car as well.

That was the third time within a month police pulled me over for an identity check. I felt harassed. None of my classmates had ever been pulled over so often in a month, if not in their entire life.

Thursday, March 20, 2003: diary entry

I had a fight last weekend and won by unanimous decision. My opponent was strong. On Sunday, I'll participate in an advanced training camp of the Amateur Boxing

Association ... Today, the Iraq War started. I'm shocked. I can't write. Nothing is to be heard in our house except the Arabic news anchor reports and the sound of bombs exploding. I'll go downstairs to my father now. My mother left the house. She can't stand us watching the news.

WEDNESDAY, APRIL 30, 2003

When I entered our house after school, my mother, once again, tried to escape to the basement. Tired of her behavior, I confronted her.

"Why are you still avoiding me?" I asked.

"I don't. It's your imagination," she said with one foot on the basement stairs.

"It's not. What is your problem?"

She looked over me and raised her head, "You decided against me and for your father."

"No," I said. "I made a religious decision for myself. This was my right, and you're still my mother. I rather think you have abandoned me because of my religious decision."

"Yeah sure. I've got no place in this family anyway. I should just run away and drive against a tree. You all would finally get rid of me," she said.

I felt guilty every time she threatened to commit suicide, allegedly because of us, and yet, I did not know how to take away her death wishes.

"Nobody wants that you do this," I said and paused, trying to understand, once again. "What does religion have to do with the fact that we have a bond as mother and son?" I asked.

She turned her back on me and walked downstairs.

She was unwilling to accept my personal freedom. Once more, I felt helpless and desperate. *How could I ever fix the relationship with my mother without denying who I was?*

June 2003: diary entry

Sophia had her confirmation in mid-May. It still feels wrong how her confirmation tears apart our family. My mother did not tell us when she signed her up for confirmation classes last winter. My father was in Iraq at that time. When he came back, he called in a family conference because of my mother's procedure. They yelled at each other for more than one hour. It was horrible. "At least one child shall be as I am—a Christian. This is my right as a mother. You have all your children on your side. She'll be on my side. I am responsible for her," she shouted. "Well then, if you both don't need me, you are not my wife anymore," he shouted back. The argument continued on and on.

On Sophia's confirmation day, he participated in the church ceremony, but didn't join us in the restaurant, as a sign of protest. I felt sorry for Sophia. Her father should have completely accompanied her on this important, identity forming, once-in-a-lifetime event.

Manal and Nour refused to show up at all. "According to Islam, Sophia should have inherited Baba's religion," they told me on the phone. I didn't agree with them. No verse of the Quran states that a child inherits the Islamic belief if the father is Muslim. Instead, the Quran says that there is no coercion in Islam. Thus, no one should ever be forced to be a Muslim.

Being a Muslim is rather a matter of will and of behavior. Being a Muslim is about showing love to Allah, to Allah's creation, to people, and to oneself.

The passive-aggressive way my father, Manal, and Nour advocate Islam resembles the politicized Islam that has been developed by people after the Prophet to propagate alleged rights and increase power for an exclusive group. It's "human-made," not holy. It's grounded in the human greed for power. It's an oppressive sin like any other politicized religion.

I find it sad how politicized religion is ripping my family to pieces. Sophia suffers most from the separation. She still cries sometimes. I've tried to comfort and distract her. Sometimes, I take her to my boxing club to work out together. I love Sophia. Her happiness and her peace are important to me. When the Christian faith helps her achieve that, I am happy for her. I've got my faith; others have theirs. So what! It's not our business to judge others. We can only try to understand them if we want to make that effort, and it's a huge effort that usually goes beyond our human capacity. Who knows if Sophia's choice was rather a social or an individual one? Probably no one. And if Manal and Nour don't want to make any effort to understand Sophia, they should at least respect the given Islamic rules. The Quran says that we shouldn't judge others because we never know their intentions. Only Allah does. Therefore, if they truly love Sophia, they should respect her choice and stay connected with her—unconditionally.

I'm convinced, even if I don't see it now, that we can follow different religions and happily and peacefully co-exist in our family, in our communities, and in the heavens if we give more love. Moreover, if we truly want to serve Allah, God or whatever we call it, we give love with pleasure to create and cherish a good life for everyone. A life where we deeply connect with others AND give them as well as ourselves personal freedom.

In August, we'll go to Eraclea Mare. I hope Italy will once again remove the tension in my family. I hope it'll be a time free of debates about politics, culture, and religion, a time of peaceful togetherness in sunny, beautiful, and enjoyable places.

In September, I'll transfer to high school. I look forward to making new friends and having new learning opportunities. Life is wonderful after all. Through all the struggles with my neighbors, family, friends, and myself, through all the losses, all the pain and despair, I have found faith during my time at WBS. I'm thankful for what I have learned. Alhamdulillah.

III. Kastel

September 2003-June 2006

"When fall took its course"

Monday, September 1, 2003: Diary Entry

I transferred to the Friedrich Ebert Gymnasium (FEG), a high school in Frankfurt. I'm glad I decided to make a new start in an environment where diversity is taken more for granted. The openness I experienced in my class today was inspiring. When Mr. Müller, my new English teacher, asked us to introduce ourselves, I heard German, Arabic, Asian, Turkish, and American names. He didn't ask any of us "where we were originally from." Instead, we were given time to get to know each other in private talks. We talked about our hobbies, what we liked and disliked, and more. Some students were very talkative. Some rather listened attentively, like me. No one was objectified and gazed at. I like the FEG.

Tuesday, November 25, 2003

WHEN I CAME HOME FROM school, my father congratulated me for Eid al-Fitr[50]. He said he was very proud that I practiced my religion faithfully. He also wanted to hand me 100 Euros as a gift in private. I was happy about his acknowledgement, but I also felt uncomfortable about the money. *I did not fast to receive money but to serve Allah.* Besides, none of my siblings fasted, and none of them got a gift on Eid. "Thank you, but my religious practice is just between me and Allah. I don't want to receive extra treatment just because I practice my religion," I said. Nevertheless, he insisted

---

50 festival of breaking of the fast, celebrated my Muslims worldwide, marks the end of Ramadan

that I should take the money. So, I took the money to please him. I told him that I loved him, and that I appreciated his recognition.

Diary entry:

I wonder how Islam became such a thorny issue in our family ...

In Iraq, my father introduced us to Islam. He was not religious until Malik died in 1977 of heart failure. After his death, he began to read religious books and go to the mosque on a regular basis. Sometimes, he took us along. He also invited people, occasionally, to listen to Quran recitations in our living room and pray together. My mother objected to the ritual prayers back then. She did not want our living room to become a religious space, which is odd, considering that we celebrated Christmas in that room as well. Back then, I was too young to figure out the reasons for her complaints.

When we came to Germany in 1991, I gradually noticed that my mother rejected Islam overall. First, she tried to keep us away from it. When my father came in 1993, she told him not to talk with us about Islam since it would distract us from learning German. Strangely, she often added that Islam promoted the immoral idea of an-eye-for-an-eye. My father often tried to convince her of the good in Islam during their loud fights; without success, though. Today, I know that while revenge is a topic in the Quran, forgiveness and mercy weigh heavier. They are mentioned frequently and are repeatedly favored over revenge. However, only the strong and the faithful can forgive.

Anyway, in these days I do not discuss Islam with my mother for the sake of peace. I've seen how viciously my parents have quarreled about religion in divisive good religion vs. bad religion arguments, and I don't want to deal with these cherry-picking and disrespectful arguments. I practice Islam to create peace within myself, in my relationships with others, and for Allah.

My siblings, with the exception of Nour, who is under constant pressure by her conservative in-laws, seem to be more disconnected from Islam than I am. I think they're not only afraid of my mother's rejection but also of the social problems they could face as Muslims in Germany. Mamun and Alim don't practice Islam at all. They only congratulate my brothers-in-law on Eid al-Fitr and join our family dinner. Manal used to wear a headscarf in Iraq but stopped wearing it when she came to Germany. She could not stand people gazing at her. After 9/11 and the subsequent "war on terror," an escalating number of people did not only gaze at veiled women but also refused to talk with them, or give them work, or rent out a flat to them, and much more. I saw it, and I heard it not only from Muslims but also from Germans who talked and sometimes even bragged about it. I understand my siblings. We already look different. Why should we attract further negative social attention by practicing a notorious religion?

The social pressure we've often faced in Germany has had an incredible self-denying and self-destructive impact on us. We have never celebrated Eid as in Iraq anymore, with a huge barbecue, many guests, and an open-end party. Only a few Muslims live in Kastel anyway. Still, even a small Eid dinner at our house leads to a useless quarrel about religion between my parents now. It feels so wrong. Why could we celebrate different religious holidays in Iraq but not in Germany? Only because of how Islam has often been pictured in Germany—as strange, outdated, oppressive, and evil? How could we let ourselves be so manipulated if it is self-evident that not Islam but people promote and do evil? Why did we allow this painful split in our family?

I still believe that religious differences can enrich our lives, if we want, since all religions can teach us new ways. It begins with simple things like Iftar, the break of the fast at night. Since my father returned from Mecca, he organized a common Iftar in the town hall during Ramadan every year. A group of Christians and Muslims would peacefully sit together, chat, eat, and laugh. Many Christians would not only enjoy the new foods and recipes but also the humble thankfulness Muslims dedicated to Allah, a principle both religions shared even if their methods were different. Every year, some Christians invited all Muslims to join their Church ceremonies, which some Muslims, like me, did. Was our mutual curiosity and respect only pretense? I don't think so.

Thursday, January 1, 2004: diary entry

Everything has gone well the last few months. I've made new friends at the FEG. My grades are good, and I've won most of my boxing fights.

Only my family struggles again.

Three days ago, Oma Erika broke her hip when she fell in her kitchen. She underwent a lengthy surgery in Oslar hospital. After she had woken up from the anesthesia, we were allowed to visit her on the ward. Her arms were fixed on the bed rail. She was fidgeting with her hands. "Help! Where am I? I want to get out of here," she screamed. I was scared—we all were. We held her hands and stroked her hair, but we couldn't calm her down. Shortly, a doctor came in to give her a sedative shot. Tears rolled down my mother's face. Sophia was completely pale and almost threw up. My father took her out of the room. After a little while, Oma Erika stared at the ceiling, unresponsive. We didn't understand what was happening with her.

The next day, the doctors diagnosed her with senile dementia. My mother has cried a lot in the last few days. I feel so sorry for her and for Oma Erika. Tomorrow, we will bring Oma Erika to our house. She'll stay with us until we know what we can do for her.

She certainly cannot live alone anymore. Amtal belongs to the past, her growing mental weakness to the present. She often feels lost. She doesn't know who she is, who we are, and where we are. More and more things suddenly seem strange to her. I feel so sad. Our bond with Oma Erika is dwindling away. Will we soon be total strangers to each other?

Friday, February 6, 2004

We, or better who remained of our family, kept together in the midst of our new crisis. Alim had moved with his girlfriend to Mainz several months ago. He rarely visited us. He studied music and focused on his dream of becoming an artist. Sophia officially still lived with us but usually hung around outside with her friends, who were mostly dealers or drug addicts. Sometimes, we did not know for days where she stayed. She was inaccessible. I tried to talk with her and get her more connected with our family, but she seemed to hate us after all the pain she had experienced in our family. Manal and Nour looked after their families. As a result, only my parents, Mamun, and I looked after Oma Erika.

We had put up a bed for Oma Erika in the middle of our living room. In the mornings, my father looked after her while we went to school or to work. He would wash her and change her clothes. Afterward, she would walk with her walker to her small maple table at the window. He would serve her coffee and a sandwich before she would take her tablets. "I'm thankful I can help her," he told me one day. "I wish I could have helped my mother the same way," he said.

In 1996, my father's mother also fell at home in Mosul and broke her hip. The doctors did not do the surgery on her, however. Since the available amount of anesthesia was insufficient due to the sanctions, it was only given to the young and strong. The doctors thus released her from the hospital with expired painkillers to die at home. When we received the call in 1996, I saw my father crying for the first time. It had broken my heart back then; in 2004, the bitter memory returned.

Luckily, we could help Oma Erika in 2004. I usually gave my father a break in the afternoons when I came home from school. While he would go upstairs to take a nap, I would help her go to bed. Sometimes, she slept for more than one hour while I did my homework at her table. More often than not, she would have difficulties sleeping, however. "Help!" she would shout. I would sit next to her and stroke her hand. "You are in Kastel. You are Oma Erika. I am Junis, your grandson. Everything is fine," I would say. Often, it helped.

My mother usually came home from work at 5 p.m., tired. Even though we faced each other more often, we did not talk about how we could improve our relationship. *Oma Erika's illness was more urgent,* I knew. Her constant confusion and shouting overwhelmed my mother. I did not want to burden her with my needs in addition. Often, she let me look after Oma Erika, while she would disappear to the basement.

Anyway, I was thankful I could give something back to Oma Erika. She was like a mother to me. "You're kind," she repeatedly told me and grabbed my hand—despite her illness.

Saturday, February 7, 2004

Mamun came home from his work at a computer company at around 6:30 p.m. He and my parents usually looked after Oma Erika in the evening while I trained in the boxing gym in Hochheim.

Rahman, my next opponent, was rated the number one of the light welterweight division in Hesse. I worked out extremely hard since I absolutely wanted to win and qualify for the Southwest Championship.

On the fight day, however, I was deeply worried about the burdens my family had to face. In addition to Oma Erika's illness, Sophia had escaped to Mannheim the previous night to meet her new boyfriend whom she had met online. My parents were so upset that they got in the car and began to search for her while my coach picked me up for the fight.

When I sat down on the bench in the changing room, I prayed and beseeched Allah would give my family the strength to fight through our struggles and become stronger people.

Afterward, I got up. The moment I changed my clothes felt unusually intense, as if I was becoming another person, a person that wouldn't know any fear or pain. I wrapped my hands and focused on the fight. I did not want any troubles to get me distracted and weak.

The air in the changing room was full of different smells: acid, cold sweat of those who were about to fight, salty sweat of those who just returned from their fight, paired with the metallic smell of blood that either gushed from their open wounds or stuck on their leather gloves, and, above all, the sharp Japanese peppermint concentrate that *Tariq,* my coach, had dropped into my nose before he warmed me up.

I hit the pads. Blood shot though my veins like burning petrol. The cold, thick petroleum jelly on my eyebrows, on my cheeks, and on my nose felt like a protective shield, as if nothing could harm me even though I knew I could easily get hurt. *I'd have to give 100 % to survive, 120 % to win.* Off and on, a fresh breeze of air sneaked into the room through a small window and touched my hot skin. I breathed in and out—deeply concentrating.

Suddenly, someone shouted in the hallway, "Next fight, Junis Sultan, BC Hochheim." Tariq stepped up and whispered into my ear, "Go! No fear. No pain. Fight, now!" I climbed up the stairs and entered the small gym that was filled with a hundred people. All eyes turned to me while I focused on the ring. My heart was beating with full strength. I was ready to fight for my life.

I stepped inside the ring and went to my corner. After I had prayed the Surat al-Fatiha[51], the bell rang, "Ding." Its echo inflamed my passion, *four three-minute rounds of my entire physical and mental strength against an undefeated opponent.* I gave everything I had.

After the final stroke of the bell, I walked back to my corner. Tariq beamed. "You made the fight," he said. I began to feel the abrasions on my back, as if someone had whipped me with a cowhide. I had gotten them when I leaned back in the ropes, which I rarely did since I dominated him from

---

51 first chapter (*surah*) of the Quran, its seven verses (*ayat*) are a prayer for the guidance, lordship, and mercy of God

the middle of the ring with my stabbing jab. Tariq took off my headgear and my gloves. My hair was wet and warm. My muscles and my skin were hot. My heartbeat slowed down. *I had no scratch on my face.* Slowly, I felt like becoming a normal human being again. People were cheering my name, people in the first row I knew and strangers in the back, too. I smiled and felt respected by the spectators.

Tuesday, March 2, 2004: diary entry

It's midnight. I'm sitting on our couch. My father is lying in front of me—in Oma Erika's bed. His eyes are closed, but he can't sleep. He's still in pain. I can see it in his face. We picked him up today, around noon, after his 11-day hospitalization. In the early morning, we brought Oma Erika to an old folks' home. I'm so sorry for her. She used to look after us with all her heart, and now we send her to such an unfamiliar place. We just can't look after two patients. It's too much for us ...

It was Friday, February 20, after my father had accompanied me to the boxing training. I was sitting right here that night, watching the news when my father entered the room, pale. "I had a lot of blood in the stool," he said. My mother drove him to the Bad Soden hospital right away. He underwent two emergency surgeries. The doctors removed an aggressive, intestinal tumor. His scar on his stomach is eight inches long. He has lost more than 30 pounds. He is still almost too weak to speak.

Wednesday, March 3, 2004: diary entry

I have to confess something awful. After the second surgery, the doctors told us that my father would probably have only two weeks to live, and that they would still try chemotherapy. I felt totally desponded. I thought I was losing my last confidant in my family. After the deadly message, I skipped school and stayed at home. I was in my room, alone. I felt so depressed, so devastated, so lost ... that I cut my arm with a knife. I don't know why I did it. I didn't think anything. I just put a bandage on my wounded arm, packed my gym bag, and went to Hochheim. After working out for two hours, I felt completely dizzy. I lurched to the changing room to take off my blood-soaked bandage. Raid, my sparring partner, entered the room after me. He gazed at my forearm with large eyes. "What happened?" he asked. I told him. "You're crazy. You mustn't do that!" he said. He's right. Why did I hurt myself? Why did I make such a horrible mistake? Have I completely lost all self-love?

Friday, March 30, 2004: diary entry

When I came home from school, I found my mother sitting in the kitchen crying. She told me that Sophia had just burned her forearms with cigarettes, and that she would send her to a locked psychiatric ward since all our family problems overburdened her. I went upstairs to Sophia and saw her arms. With tears in my eyes, I hugged her for a long moment.

I'm so sick with regret. What happened is my fault. No one noticed that I had cut my arm, except Sophia. Tears are rolling down my face ... Oh Allah, I don't want to lose courage. Please, give me the strength to prevail. I'll fight for my family. I'll support and listen. I'll do the housework. I'll do everything I can. I want to be a pillar and not a disaster.

Monday, April 26, 2004: Diary entry

Sophia is still locked up. Two days ago, she burned her forearms again. When we visited her, she threw my mother's flowers in a dustbin and ran away. The psychiatrist says that her problem is rooted in our family's cultural conflicts, that she is torn between the two sides and thus lacks a feeling of belonging and emotional security. Is her psychiatrist right? I guess so. Often, I think and feel the same way. Do I allow it to destroy me? It seems.

Yesterday, I felt this inner strife, this ripping pain, and empty brokenness again. We brought Oma Erika to us for her 88th birthday. We had many German visitors. They drank champagne, ate pork-sandwiches, and talked about German folk music. They had things in common, while I felt left out. On the other hand, I repeatedly notice that I'm far from being an "Iraqi" either, especially when I'm with my brothers-in-law. I'm so sick of thinking about it ...

It could be worse, I often tell myself. Be thankful that you don't live in war, I often tell myself. It's a shame that you're so hypersensitive, I often tell myself. This is how I go on, knowing that I'm still lost. How can I connect with anyone if I don't love myself? How can I love myself again if I have, from early on, repeatedly been taught to hate myself? How deep is this self-hate embedded in my soul? The self-satisfaction I experienced over the years has been only superficial. I was satisfied when I was good at school and in good shape, but it has never given me a deep happiness and peace of mind.

END OF APRIL 2004: DIARY ENTRY

People need to connect. That's how we are wired. And people need to be free to be who they are and want to be. That's how we are wired. Otherwise, we get sick.

SATURDAY, MAY 1, 2004: DIARY ENTRY

It doesn't make sense to be depressed, self-pitying, and afraid of failing in life because it leads to failure here and now. I've missed more than 50 class hours, and I can hardly catch up now. I was barely admitted to the 12th grade because of *high absences. Stop! I mustn't destroy myself. I am responsible for my life. I'll focus on school again. Education is my ticket for a better future. With a good high school diploma, I could go to the university.*

Wednesday, May 5, 2004

Before my father got ill at the end of February, my parents had planned to build a bungalow in our backyard for Oma Erika. Her illness made them work together again after they had given each other the silent treatment in the aftermath of Sophia's confirmation. They gave our architect full freedom of planning, which led to a surprising outcome.

One day, we received the suggested construction plan. My father handed me the folder after school. I looked through the plan of a 1,400-square-foot family house and smiled, hopeful. *Building had bound my parents together in 1997. It could do the same in 2004.*

In fact, their relationship was already improving. When he stayed in the hospital for 11 days, she cried almost every day. One day, during our teatime, she said she could not live without him. The way she said it sounded like she still loved him after all.

Saturday, June 26, 2004: diary entry

Lots of good news! My father's chemotherapy is completed. The doctors say he is healed. Alhamdulillah! He also applied to build that house in our backyard. The new house will improve our living conditions. Alhamdulillah! Further, Oma Erika lives here with us again. She is doing okay. Alhamdulillah! Finally yet importantly, Sophia was released two days ago. She feels better now. Alhamdulillah!

Tomorrow, we'll all go to Italy for our summer vacation. The fresh ocean breeze, the salty water, and the warm sun will nurture our bodies and souls!

Friday, October 1, 2004

Back in Kastel, we received the building permit from the authorities.

On October 1, I watched the demolition work before I went to school. Frankfurter Weg, the street behind our backyard, was cordoned off. A mechanical digger evacuated the organic waste and the ruins of our garage with a rumbling noise that awakened our neighborhood. I was excited and even somewhat proud. *We more than just settled in Kastel. We were already building our second, new house*—a big achievement in our neighborhood. Even though I knew it was only a materialistic success, optimism captured me. *Our new house could be more than just stones. It could be a place free of harassment from a xenophobic neighbor, a place where we could appreciate one another and ourselves, a place we could gladly call our home.*

Monday, October 4, 2004

The school bell rang for the break. I went down to the cafeteria. My friends were already sitting in front of the counter. I shook hands with *Payam,* my sparring partner from Frankfurt, then with *Samir, Sebastian, Andrej, Justina, Dorothee,* and Helena. We were all either in the same English or PE advanced course. Usually, I sat and talked with them, but that day I was so tired from my last workout that I excused myself. I walked to a free table in the back of the dining hall to have a nap.

As I sat down, I saw the girl who had been watching me with her big, brown eyes, hiding behind her girlfriends when I had entered the cafeteria. She stood up from her table. We looked at each other, unrestrained. She had straight, brown hair, a thin nose, and a well-developed figure. I felt intrigued and yet so tired that I lay my head on the table and slowly closed my eyes.

After a little while, I sensed someone close to me. I opened my eyes. *She* was standing in front of me, smiling. She asked for my name. I told her.

"Beautiful name. I like it," she paused. "Are you Arab?" she asked and immediately added, "I'm sorry, I'm just always so curious. You don't have to tell!"

"Well, half; and half-German, if you want to see me that way," I said, somewhat irritated by her question.

"Wow! German?" She laughed. "I would never have thought."

"I believe you," I said. "And what's your name, if I may ask?"

"Ceylin," she said and smiled again.

I liked her kind way.

"That's a beautiful name, too. It's Turkish, right?" I said before I noticed that I had gotten myself into the same guessing game even though I believed that the question of ethnicity shouldn't be immediately asked when meeting someone new. *It says nothing about a person anyway.* Instead, I wanted to know who Ceylin really was.

"Right. It means the door to heaven."

I believed every word she said.

"Well, I have to go. I'll certainly see you around here again, right?" she said.

"Yeah," I said, playing cool even though I was already falling for her. I wanted to see her again, rather sooner than later. *What a woman! So charming and humorous. Out of nowhere, she had just entered my life and easily made me smile.*

Thursday, October 7, 2004

School ended at 4 p.m. I rode home on my yellow Gilera SP 50 scooter. Before I could enter the house, I heard my parents shouting. Alarmed, I quietly opened the front door.

"I've never been accepted by anyone of your family in Iraq," she shouted.

"What about Ammu Nuri? He loved you and always cared for you. And my father was proud of you, too," he shouted back.

"And your mother said that I was good-for-nothing and only a cheap European whore."

"I told you many times, don't talk like that about my mother!"

"I can say what I want. I've always been the one who was abused, and everyone who has ever abused me will pay for it here and on judgment day."

"Woe! Are you still talking about my mother?" he shouted with a raised finger while I briefly glanced into the kitchen.

"I'm talking about you and everyone else in this family. I'll move out. I can't bear living here any longer. No one respects me."

She pushed me aside and ran to the front door.

He followed her, shouting, "Yeah, go! Nobody can stand your constant need to fight anyway. You just argue because Ramadan is coming and you want to ruin the atmosphere."

She banged the door. My heart was racing. *Why could they not just get along?*

After a short while, he came to the kitchen and told me in a normal voice, "We've got rice and tomato sauce with zucchini, eggplant, and ground meat."

I put some food on my plate and sat down, upset and aware. *His and Oma Erika's illness did not improve their relationship at all.* "Why were you quarreling again?" I asked.

"Because I was listening to a Quran CD while I was cooking your food. I thought she would be at work until 5 p.m., but she came home earlier. When she opened the door and heard the recitations, she started to shout at me. She doesn't want Quran recitations in our house."

I shook my head and swallowed. "She can't forbid us to be Muslim. I mean, what are you going to do about it? Do you want to accept her behavior? She married you as a Muslim."

"I don't accept it, but I'm also tired of arguing. I listen to Quran citations when she isn't at home, and when she is here, I don't. I just try not to provoke her."

"I think that's the wrong strategy. We have supported and accommodated her religious practice. We celebrated Christian holidays with her, like Christians, including listening to Christian music for weeks. We don't say anything when she eats pork or puts rum in her tea. It doesn't even come to my mind to overplay our differences. So what about our rights? Are we not free to choose and practice our religion?"

"It's not that easy with her. You know that better than any of your siblings do."

"And it's still wrong," I insisted and looked at his distraught face. "Look, I'll go back to school now and meet a friend." I paused. "Baba, don't worry too much. It won't change a thing. You should tell her that she needs to accept your freedom as well."

He sighed and looked at me as if he was considering my thoughts.

I went upstairs and quickly got ready for my first date with Ceylin. I changed, brushed my teeth, and put Hugo Boss Bottled[52] on my neck.

---

52 perfume

We had exchanged numbers the other day. Since then, Ceylin texted me frequently. She made me forget about all problems at home. She made me feel appreciated and special.

Smiling, I took my helmet and left at full throttle to meet her in Frankfurt.

She was standing at the entrance of the yellow train station. Through the visor, I could see how she smiled when she spotted my scooter. I parked next to the bicycle stand and took off my helmet. We slowly met halfway while people hectically moved around us.

"You know what I have noticed?" she said with shiny eyes. "You used to look so serious, but since we have gotten to know each other, you can suddenly smile. Why?"

"It's because I'm happy to be with you," I said.

We looked into each other's eyes. My heart pounded. I was thrilled.

"Where can we go? I don't want you to get into trouble with your relatives for hanging out with me," I said, anticipating that she was a Muslim and that our date could be a risk.

As a cultural rule among rather radical Muslims, dating and getting to know the other sex before marriage was not allowed without the presence of a third person. The rule intends to keep Muslims' chastity, which is demanded in the Quran. I considered this cultural rule, not because I believed that our date would lead to premarital sexual intercourse and hellfire, but because I wanted to protect Ceylin from bad-mouthing and more serious consequences by her relatives, who I did not know yet. I would never have allowed sexual intercourse on our first dates anyway. I wanted to get to know Ceylin in depth.

She looked at me, smiled, and replied, "I appreciate your thoughtfulness. We shouldn't go to the central shopping area. My aunt works there. What about the River Main?"

"Great," I said, believing that it was a wonderful haven to get to know each other. Grassland, meandering footways, and tall trees next to a white church led down to the river.

As we walked down the park, we talked about our hobbies and our wishes for the future. Even though I did not speak as much as she did, she was interested in every word I said. She seemed to be fascinated by who I was, and she captivated me as well.

After we had passed the 600-year-old church, we walked along the riverside to a small playground. "Let's stay for a while. I used to play here," she said. She began to swing, like a child that happily enjoyed the moment of getting higher and higher. I was inspired by her light-heartedness. *There was something in her smile,* I sensed, *which I had lost a long time ago.* I sat down on the swing next to her. "Come on!" she said excitedly. Soon, we began to race. We could not stop laughing until we stopped to swing. In a gentle manner, we began to talk about our childhood. When I told her that the first four years of my childhood ended abruptly with war, her understanding eyes showed me how much she was able to empathize.

At sunset, we began to walk back. Before we reached the busy crowd at the train station, we stopped underneath a plane tree. *It was time to say goodbye.* We looked into each other's eyes. "I'm glad I have met you," she said and smiled. I smiled back, "I'm glad to hear that. You already know how happy I am to be with you." Speechless, we continued our walk.

At the train station, I told her that we should meet again soon.

"Yes, please! I'll see you tomorrow at school, right?" she asked.

I smiled and nodded before I jumped on my scooter and drove away.

Back home, I carried my cell phone with me all the time. I could not stop thinking of her, but I also did not want to push too much after our first date. I was lying in my bed with my white Sony Ericsson cell phone underneath my pillow when she texted me around 10 p.m. She wished me a good night. I replied. At 2:30 a.m., she texted me again. "Can you sleep?" I replied with a blissful smile. I loved her direct and honest way.

Friday, October 8, 2004

When she entered the cafeteria, our eyes met for a short, intense moment. Yet, we did not approach each other. We did not want the others to know about us since it could have meant trouble. *They could tell her family about us,* which we, unspoken, wanted to prevent.

At the end of our break, she asked her friends if they had done their chemistry homework. Since none of them had, she came to me and asked if she could have my folder. While we attended different courses, we were taught by the same teacher. Secretly glad that I could help her, I gave her my folder. We smiled for a second before she headed off.

I remained seated and pondered for a moment. *Could we ever act like the other couples at the FEG? Christian couples were usually not subject to strict rules and constrictions.* Jörg and Kathy of my English course, for instance, often held hands and kissed each other in public. The FEG counted many couples like them. Non-Muslim-girl-and-Muslim-boy couples were rare since Muslims constituted a minority. *Yet, these couples usually enjoyed more freedom as well,* like Helena and Aziz, her Turkish boyfriend. Muslim boys, contrary to Muslim girls, were often given more freedom in terms of sexuality by their parents as long as their girlfriends were non-Muslims. *As if non-Muslim girls had less honor than Muslim girls,* who were expected to remain virgins until their wedding night. *And as if Muslim boys fucking non-Muslim girls for fun were not a sin.* I was still a virgin in 2004. Yet, *sex before marriage was okay for me if it came with love and the intention to stay together.*

The longer I thought about everything, the more I realized how lucky Ceylin and I were. *Our relationship was matchless and incredibly intense. It was neither easy nor phony. It was just between us—the perfection of intimate togetherness.*

Sunday, October 10, 2004

Ceylin had to lie to her parents to be with me. She told them she would visit *Derya,* her best friend, while in reality she drove to Kastel.

I awaited her at the Park and Ride (P&R) at sundown. She was smiling all over her face when she got out of her mother's car and so was I. "I like your perfume!" she said. My neck smelled like citrus and sweet cinnamon with a touch of santal and vetiver. "Thank you," I said. "I only use it on special occasions." We both laughed, sweetly concerned, as if time was on our side and yet against us. We knew, *she could not stay very long.*

We began to walk on the bikeway next to the thicket along the railways. Long, ovate, and serrated leaves in red, yellow, and brown colors crunched under our feet. Leaves were also floating from the sky while the golden sun was setting. Fall took its course.

"What a beautiful day!" I said. I deeply breathed in the cool air.

She stopped. I stopped as well. We looked into each other's eyes.

"I know that I want you and no one else," she said.

I got goose bumps from her openness. For a second, I thought about what to say, but then I lost and found myself again in her eyes. I was becoming like Ceylin—a free heart. "And I want you and no one else," I said. My lips came closer to hers. We closed our eyes. I kissed her tender lips. A sweeping warmth captured my chest. She kissed me gently and passionately at the same time while I found a kindred spirit in her strong and complex emotionality.

Love was alive.

Wednesday, October 13, 2004

The foundation of Frankfurter Weg 7 was poured when I came from school. I took a picture with my cell phone. I appreciated every step it took to build our house.

Friday, October 15, 2004

Like the previous days, Ceylin and I met in the underground garage ten minutes before the first lesson started. I drove down the ramp and parked across from the staircase, where she was waiting for me. We smiled at each other. I walked to her and gave her a kiss.

"Why do I only get a quick kiss today?" she asked.

"Ramadan started. We should not kiss. I'm fasting," I said.

"Yes, it started, and I'm fasting, too," she looked at me, puzzled.

"We should behave decently, especially in Ramadan."

"But according to Islam, we're not even allowed to kiss till we're married."

"I know, but there is no compulsion in religion, and I interpret Islam in a liberal way. Our intention is good. We love each other, and we want to stay together."

"Then kiss me like you used to."

"I don't want to kiss you when I've got bad breath."

She grabbed my hands and said, "I don't care about that, Junis."

I looked at her serious face but found it hard not to smile. "Why don't we kiss decently during the day like we just did? What can be wrong about showing love to each other as long as we don't go wild? And at night when we don't fast, when we taste better, I'll kiss you as I used to. Would that be okay for you my love?"

She smiled back, "I was afraid you wouldn't want to kiss me for a month now."

"You know I could never have done that," I said.

We laughed, both relieved, before she went up the staircase, and I walked up the ramp.

Wednesday, October 20, 2004

The basement was built in the afternoon. I enjoyed watching the construction. The walls came in heavy, pre-assembled, armored concrete plates. In contrast to the walls of Paul-Ehrlich-Straße 4, our new house was solid.

End of October 2004

Ceylin and I still behaved carefully in public to not get into trouble with her family. By the end of October, however, some of our close friends noticed that we were a couple. Our eyes revealed our secret. Still, I knew I could count on my friends. They did not speak about us.

One day, Ceylin and I briefly met after our art course behind the staircase. I was wearing a T-shirt. We were talking about our next date when her look suddenly froze. I tried to quickly hide my arm, but it was too late. "Junis, what's that on your arm?" she asked, concerned.

I felt tense. I had no idea what to tell her. I myself did not even know why I had cut my arm. Moreover, I did not want to make up a story like so often when people asked me about the scars.

One day, Helena asked me as well. I told her that I fell in a ditch with spiky roots. Of course, she did not believe me. She said I could talk to her anytime, but I always felt too embarrassed to talk about the scars.

To Ceylin, however, I wanted to tell the truth as far as I could.

"An accident," I said.

"Did you cut yourself?"

I nodded, regretful.

She grabbed my arm and looked at it. "Why?"

"I don't really know. I had a lot of problems, and I was weak."

She let my arm go and stepped back, "How can I know you won't cut yourself the next time you're in trouble?"

"If I could undo one thing, it'd be these scars," I said. "I made a stupid mistake. It's haram to hurt oneself. The body is a gift from Allah. I will never do it again."

"I will have to believe you," she said.

Yet, I could see that she was still shaken, and I understood.

"Let's meet in Kastel tonight," I paused. "Give me a chance to explain myself. I know it's difficult to understand such crazy behavior, but let me try to explain everything."

She came at 9 p.m. We were sitting in her car when I told her about the traumas I faced at an early age and the fears I developed thereafter. I told her about the war, the losses, the discrimination, the early abuse by my mother, my fear of rejection and abandonment, my parents' constant fights, the recurring feeling of being torn, Oma Erika's and my father's sudden illnesses, and how I was, at one point, completely overwhelmed by helplessness, despair, and apathy, which somehow made me cut my arm, as if the physical pain could take away the emotional pain. I had never told anyone about it, and I hoped she would understand.

After I had told her everything, she held my head with her hands. With tears in her eyes, she said, "You'll never stand alone from now on because I am on your side." I felt accepted, embraced, and even protected, *as if nothing could harm me anymore.*

Thursday, November 11, 2004

The walls of the first floor were built with white, aerated concrete bricks. I watched the workers occasionally while I did my homework at Oma Erika's table. We kept Oma Erika in a nearby old people's home for the period of the building since the noise would have frightened her too much. We visited her every day. She was doing okay.

Sunday, November 14, 2004

Ceylin and I met every other night in Kastel until Eid al-Fitr when she asked if she could come around 8 p.m. I told her that I would first have to ask my father since we had my family over.

I approached him in the kitchen.

"It's Eid al-Fitr, the end of Ramadan. What friend do you want to invite? Our family is together tonight," he said.

"She's a friend from high school," I said.

"A girl? A Muslim?" he asked, suspicious.

Suddenly, Ammu Serhat joined up with us. He was listening to our talk from the living room. "Where does she come from?" he asked me.

"Her parents are from Turkey," I said, irritated by his question.

"I don't know if that's a good idea," he said and looked at my father.

"What about her parents? Is she not with her family on Eid?" my father asked me.

"They already ate, and she was allowed to go out and celebrate with her friends," I said.

He pondered for a moment before he said, "If it's like that, she can come."

I smiled, happy about his decision and looking forward to seeing her.

The elders have to be respected and honored in Islam. Ammu Serhat thus did not dare to contradict him. In contrast to my family, apart from my mother and Sophia, I did not believe in this religious rule unconditionally after I had experienced how many Muslims interpreted it. Often, it meant that almost whatever the elders said or did, even if it was wrong, the youth had to respect and honor it. I often wondered how this practice could build honest, progressive relationships and societies. Nonetheless, that night, I had made use of that rule to bypass my brothers-in-law, anticipating that my father would be more open to Ceylin's and my rather benign wish.

I walked upstairs. Shortly after I had texted Ceylin that she could come, Ammu Serhat confronted me in my room. "Junis, that girl, are you dating her, or is she just a friend?"

I was surprised at myself that I did not mind his judgment anymore. I felt confident with my father and Ceylin on my side. "I'm dating her."

"My brother, be careful. I think you're making a severe mistake."

"Why do you think so? We like each other a lot."

"Akhi,[53] listen. Your sister and I have experienced cold treatment in Turkey. In addition, I know many Turks here. If you don't know Turkish, the Turks cheat you."

---

53 Arabic, means "my brother"

"First, *they* are not all the same. Second, we speak German. Third, I can learn Turkish."

"What about her parents? Do they know you?"

"No. We are keeping it a secret for the time being."

"Believe me. I know a lot of Turks. You can get in big trouble if her family finds out."

"I know that. That's why we're careful."

He shook his head and left the room.

She came to the P&R at 8 p.m. We congratulated each other for the end of Ramadan with a kiss.

I sensed that she was nervous, "Are you okay?"

"Yes, but maybe we should wait to meet your family until we are engaged," she said.

"Don't worry about them. If my father says yes, nobody can say anything."

"All right then," she said and followed me.

I walked her to the living room, where my family was sitting on the couch. Everyone stared at us with large eyes. I introduced her as a friend from school.

"Selam, all the best for Bayram!" she said to my family.

Ammu Serhat and Ammu Amir congratulated her in Arabic, "Kul Aam wa antum bi-Khair.[54]"

Manal added, "You say Bayram for Eid in Turkey, right?"

Ceylin nodded and turned red, "Yes."

"It's basically the same," I said to my family, irritated by their looks and their linguistic and nationalistic games.

---

54 means "may you be well every year"

"So, you attend the same school," my mother said.

"Correct. Your son is a good student," Ceylin replied.

"I know," she muttered, examining Ceylin from head to toe.

I felt embarrassed. *Was she dismissive because she anticipated that Ceylin was a Muslim?* I wanted to free Ceylin and wondered, at the same time, how my mother could know about my grades if she refused to look at my report cards since I had become a Muslim.

Meanwhile, Ammu Amir and Ammu Serhat kept staring at Ceylin and me. I assumed I knew what their problem was—*me inviting a girl on Eid without engagement and on top not an Iraqi but a Turkish girl.*

Despite feeling annoyed, I behaved calmly. I did not want to argue and humiliate everyone even more. *It was not worth it. My mother and my brothers-in-law would probably never tolerate Ceylin and me since we did not fit into their limited view of life.* I walked Ceylin to the kitchen. My father followed us, "Tell Ceylin she shouldn't feel ashamed. She can take anything. If she wants something else, she can tell you." Since she did not want to eat anything, I asked him if we could go upstairs. He nodded. Ceylin and I smiled. I was glad we could escape their bold looks and comments.

Wednesday, December 1, 2004

Ceylin and I were sitting in the cafeteria during our free period, back to back.

While our friends were talking with each other, she whispered to me, "Let's go to my family's new house! No one is there now."

"I don't think that's a good idea," I whispered back.

"Come on! I wouldn't take you there if there were a chance they could see us."

I hesitated and pondered. *What if someone else saw us together, a neighbor, or anyone who could tell her parents? Could Ceylin say that I was just a classmate who came to pick up something? Were her parents maybe not as radical as we expected? Would they possibly even like me?* Somehow, I believed that everything would be okay. On top, I knew how proud Ceylin was of their new house. She loved drawing and wanted to become an architect one day, like her uncle who had planned the house. I wanted to do her this favor.

"But if we go, we won't stay long," I said.

"Sure, I'll just show you our new house and my new room."

We left the school grounds together, for the first time, to walk to her house. It had a pitched, red roof. Ceylin and her family lived on the first floor. The other three floors were rented out.

She showed me around in the first floor before we entered her room, which was bright and beautiful. White curtains covered the huge floor windows. While we walked on the maple flooring, the curtains waved in the wind. The windows were tilted. A fresh breeze touched our faces. We sat down on her white, king-sized bed. Mild sunbeams were shining on us as we began to kiss.

After a while, we opened our eyes.

She laughed, "Your eyes got small again."

"What?" I said, alarmed. I got up, "Let's go!"

"Just a little bit more."

"No," I said. *I had lost the sense of time while we were together.*

Wednesday, December 8, 2004

The shell construction of our three-story house was finished. Since our neighbors refused to let us exceed the mandatory ten-foot distance to the property boundaries, our house was built in a long form. The floor areas contained 50 square meters. Each floor was neatly arranged. Our house was still big enough for a family with three children.

Sunday, December 12, 2004: diary entry

Ceylin hasn't come to school for more than a week. I've called her a couple of times, but she didn't pick up. Three days ago, she texted me, "I've got problems at home." I asked her what had happened, but she didn't reply. Last night, she texted me, "I can't talk." I was so upset that I got in my mother's car and drove toward Frankfurt through lightning, thunder, and heavy rain. When I entered an intersection, I hydroplaned and almost hit a silver Mercedes that was stopped at the traffic light. Fortunately, I only hit the traffic *light. I reversed and drove back home with a broken axis, a distorted bumper, broken front lights, and a collateral bump on the driver's door. "The main thing is nobody got hurt," my mother said, startled. CEYLIN, TALK WITH ME! I'M GOING CRAZY WITHOUT YOU.*

Saturday, January 8, 2005

I knew that Ceylin worked at Woolworth in the shopping area. Even though she had warned me to never visit her since she worked with her aunt, I asked Piero to give me a ride. I could not wait any longer. I wanted to know what was going on.

I entered the store at 7:40 p.m. and approached Ceylin at the cash register.

"I told you not to come here!" she whispered to me angrily.

"I won't leave until you tell me what is going on," I whispered.

"Okay, go! Wait outside!" she said.

I waited outside next to some T-shirt stands, tense. After ten minutes, a saleswoman wheeled in the stands. At 8 p.m., she closed the shop while Ceylin began to count the cash.

At 8:15 p.m., Ceylin came outside. We walked to a dark corner next to the shop door.

"I've got no time. Only five minutes," she said, stressed.

"Ceylin, what's going on? I've been trying to reach you for almost a month. Don't you remember? We wanted to be there for one another. Let me help you."

She looked to the ground, "You help me when you leave me alone."

"You mean for good and all?" I asked in disbelief. "Say it in my face."

She raised her head. Tears rolled down her cheeks. "My parents found out about us."

I looked at her, taken aback. Even though I had been afraid of this reality for a month, I had always told myself that we had been careful enough, that there would be other issues in her family, anything but not that. "Why didn't you tell me?" I said quietly.

"Because my father took away my cell phone. I'm not allowed to contact you anymore," she said. "If we continue to meet, I'll be married to someone else."

I suddenly felt a heavy pressure on my chest. "But we're young adults now. Aren't we free to love?"

"No. My father wants me to marry a Turk," she said.

Her words felt like invisible blades stabbed in my heart. I had not seen it coming. "But I'm a Muslim, like you and your family. Isn't that good enough?"

She shook her head. "No."

That moment, my world fell apart. *Ceylin and I were lost.* Tears filled my eyes. "If it's like that, we're not a couple anymore," I said in a trembling voice.

"I think that's the best for everyone."

"No, it's not. You're wrong. And your father is wrong, too. It doesn't matter, though, because you have already decided against us."

Silent tears streamed down our faces.

"I've got to go now. Goodbye," she said and left.

My legs were shaking. I was standing in the dark, watching her walk away under orange shining street lamps until she disappeared behind a corner house.

I lurched to Piero's car, which was parked on a side street in the dark—looking back.

"Come on, that bitch is gone. Get in the car now!" Piero shouted.

I passed a metal trashcan and punched it so hard that it got a dent. The lights in the houses around us came on. Piero rapidly got out of his car.

"Are you okay? Get in the damn car. Let's go now," he said.

I sat down on the passenger seat and looked at him, devastated.

"She's not a bitch," I paused. "I love her. What the hell have I done?"

"What happened?"

"We ended it. It wasn't in our hands anymore."

"Champ, life's a bitch, and we need to be strong." He switched on the engine and drove me home.

TUESDAY, JANUARY 11, 2005: DIARY ENTRY

She's gone. The most horrible sentence I have ever written. What is waiting for me now? Insanity and self-destruction? Forbidden feelings and torturing memories tear me down day and night. I look into the mirror and see a wreck: dark circles around the eyes, oily hair, a three-day-old beard, and still heavy tears in my eyes. Who understands how I feel? Nobody. No student I know has ever been forced out of a relationship by parents. Who am I in this world? I feel like a nobody.

Monday, February 21, 2005

My parents went to the notary to register Frankfurter Weg 7 as part of the Paul-Ehrlich-Straße 4 property. Both houses were written in my mother's name. I took notice of it without interest. My mind and my body were completely occupied by Ceylin.

Sunday, February 27, 2005: diary entry

I'm falling. I see neither beginning nor end. At a lethal pace, I'm falling in the dark—trying to catch something, but I feel nothing. Ceylin, my wonderful bond, is destroyed.

I haven't prayed since we broke up. I lost my motivation to practice religion. What should I pray for if I already ended up in hell? There is no shelter for me, no mercy, no hope. Ceylin is carved into my bleeding heart. Happiness and peace have never been so far away. All I wanted was one person who loved me. All I wanted was somebody to love. Why can't I simply have Ceylin, my love? How can this torture ever be good for me, ya Allah? Where are you? Is this hell really what you have planned for me?

Piero parked in front of Paul-Ehrlich-Straße 4 around 10 p.m. He honked the horn a dozen times before he shouted from the street, "Junis. Come out! It's me, Piero. I know you're at home; I just talked to your father. You need to get out. I'll wait until you come out."

While he continued to shout, my father knocked on my room door.

"I don't want to see anyone anymore," I said in a low voice.

"Junis, habibi, what happened? I feel so sorry for you. Please, let me help you. Piero wants to help you, too. He's waiting for you outside," he paused. "We love you."

He waited in front of my door.

However, nobody and nothing mattered to me anymore. "Please, just leave me alone," I said.

I was lying on my bed, gazing at the poster of Mecca on my ceiling. Thousands of Muslims circled the Kaaba. Suddenly, the picture seemed to become real. I imagined walking with unknown people. Close-up: a teardrop of mine fell down in slow motion, growing bigger and bigger until it hit the ground and created an ocean. I began to fight against raging waves. Suddenly, reality hit me full force. The loss of Ceylin captured my entire life. *Brotherhood seemed to exist only in the theory of Islam,* I thought. *Even the closest Muslims in my life considered me not good enough. I remained an unwanted creature in a heartless and mindless world of random, human-made separations.* My faith was smashed. Tears rolled down my cheeks.

Friday, March 11, 2005: diary entry

Why do her parents not give us a chance? Why do they have so much power over her? Or maybe does she share their view? Why then did she date me in the first place? Or is she afraid of her family, of being rejected, persecuted, or even killed for being with someone like me? Is her family really that cruel? Or are they pressured by their relatives to get her married to a Turk? Did she hope she would find a spirit of rebellion within herself against her family? Why then did she lose her courage? What about our dream of togetherness and happiness?

Today, her friends told me that her father engaged her to a Turk already in December 2004. I had thought only death could bring us apart. It was much less, though. It was our cowardice to fight for our dream. What cowards we were, what cowards we are.

Saturday, March 12, 2005

After three months of depression and comfort eating, I forced myself to lose 15 pounds in a week to box in the light welterweight division for which Tariq had registered me. I thought boxing would help me forget about her.

It was my 17th bout. My opponent, *Hartmann,* was a national league boxer. He had had more than 70 bouts. Since I had lost against him by split decision a year ago, I knew that I would have to put him under a lot of pressure and get into infighting to defeat him.

I pushed too hard in the first round. In the second round, I was too weak to oppose him any longer.

"Keep your hands up, keep them up!" Tariq shouted.

My arms were too heavy, though. Hartmann broke my nose. Next, he pushed me in the corner.

"Get out of there! Get the fuck out of there!" Tariq shouted hysterically.

However, my feet were too tired. A staggering uppercut followed—a classic knockout, the first one in my life. I got up at eight, too late and stumbling. The referee counted me out.

With a low head, I walked back to the changing room. Tariq and my father followed me. "Junis," Tariq said carefully, but I was already losing myself. "Ahhhhh!" I shouted, punching against the locker, again and again. Tariq and my father quietly left the room.

Friday, July 8, 2005: diary entry

I have rarely seen Ceylin at school for months now. Today, Helena told me in the cafeteria that Ceylin got married. SHE GOT MARRIED!

I hate myself. And I hate her pseudo-religious, nationalistic father even more. Look what love has done! How low have I become? Has love really led me to self-loathing and hating another person, or is it rather that I am the problem myself?

Wednesday, August 18, 2005

When I came home from school, the finishing of our new house had been completed. The first and the second stage of the facade were painted white, the third stage ocher, a unique color in our neighborhood. Our new kitchen contained high-end devices. From the window, I could see the P&R. Even though our new house was a luxury, my initial optimism was gone. The fact that our house stood directly in front of the P&R already reminded me of her—*Ceylin*.

I spent the entire evening on our roof terrace, pondering what to do with my life. My mother, Mamun, and Oma Erika stayed in Paul-Ehrlich-Straße 4 for the time being, while my father, Sophia, and I were at the point of moving into Frankfurter Weg 7.

Thursday, November 3, 2005: diary entry

What shall I do after high school? I'll certainly not do military service and support the killing of people. I'll do civil service. Today, my father told me that I could contact a friend of his in the U.S.A. who works on projects that aid developing countries. I'd like to help other people. Maybe I could carry out my civil service in the U.S.A. Since I learned about the U.S. Civil Rights Movement at WBS, I've been fascinated by the U.S. political struggles. Martin Luther King Jr's Dream still inspires me. I'm also for the pursuit of happiness, for liberty and unity, for brotherhood and acknowledging the truth that we are all created equal. I have often missed these truths in Germany.

Or maybe I failed in this society. Maybe I even failed as a human being. Maybe I am the reason why I have remained a stranger. Maybe I should have assimilated more. Even Piero got sick of my sentimental Ceylin story. He said I should just take another girl and join him partying. I can't. I still love her.

Monday, March 14, 2006: diary entry

I had a talk with my father about my plan to go to the U.S.A. Now, he suddenly changed his mind. He said I had to stay to look after the houses and after my siblings since he was too old and wouldn't have much longer to live. WHY, oh WHY does he select me to be the caretaker in the future? I don't want that role. It makes me mad. He said Manal and Nour had their family duties. So why not Mamun? Is it my fault that he's a gaming-addict? Is it my fault that Alim is a traveling artist who is always in the red? Is it my fault that Sophia is a drug-addict? What about my life? What about my dream of happiness and peace? How can I live in Germany? In cold isolation and depression like in previous years?

Wednesday, June 14, 2006

On our last school day, Mr. Müller handed out our high school diplomas in our classroom. I had a 2.5 GPA[55], a mediocre, disappointing, but well-deserved final result. After Ceylin, I had skipped school frequently. Depressed and unable to focus, I had done poorly in a couple of tests, which all counted into the final grades.

I put the diploma in my bag and left school as soon as we were dismissed. Most students stayed on the school grounds to celebrate the end of schooling, while I jumped on my scooter to run away. I was sick of school, sick of Frankfurt. Every place reminded me of her—Ceylin. I did not want to ever enter Frankfurt again.

Since my father had not allowed me to go to the U.S.A. either, I applied to do my nine-month civil service in the Hofheim hospital. I was accepted, *which was good after all, I believed. These nine months would help me figure out what I would do with my life.*

---

55 Grade Point Average

III. Kastel

July 2006-October 2007

"Life is a constant comeback"

Wednesday, July 26, 2006: Diary entry

I want to share my love but I can't because I'm alone. I can't even call our new house a home. My family is drifting further and further apart. Sophia is locked up in psychiatric ward again after she seriously burned her arms with cigarettes. Tears are rolling down my cheeks ... I tried to convince her a couple of times that hurting herself wouldn't make anything better, but I failed. I feel so guilty. I should have tried more to build her up. I thought she would manage somehow. I was wrong, though. And Mamun? Today, my father requested me again to look after him since he locks himself in his room every day after work to play "World of Warcraft." All my attempts in the last years to get him out of the house have failed, though. He doesn't want to play basketball, or rollerblade, or go for a walk, or spend time in the MTZ, or watch a movie in the cinema as we used to do in the 1990s. He's lost in the world of gaming. And my parents? Since my father moved into our new house, they have fought almost every day. My mother is tired of going between our houses, and yet she doesn't know if she wants to live with my father, either. Today, they fought so viciously that they wanted to get a divorce again. I'm so sick of it ... I wonder, why do I actually let their problems burden me all the time? I'm almost 20 years old. Isn't it time to find my own way?

Sunday, January 28, 2007: diary entry

Last night, I went to the cinema. First, it felt somewhat embarrassing because I had never gone to the cinema alone. But since I had no one to accompany me, I just went. I needed to get out of the house. I watched "Rocky Balboa," the sixth part of the film series. Since we had come to Germany, I repeatedly sought inspiration from Rocky. Rocky taught me to always keep on fighting and never give up. The new movie encouraged me once again. I got goose bumps in one particular scene. Rocky was talking to his grown-up son, and it felt as if he was talking to me. They were standing on a deserted street at night when Rocky told his son:

> "You grew up good and wonderful ... Then the time came for you to be your own man and take on the world, and you did. But somewhere along the line, you changed. You stopped being you. You let people stick a finger in your face and tell you you're no good. And when things got hard, you started looking for something to blame, like a big shadow. Let me tell you something you already know. The world ain't no sunshine and rainbows. It's a very mean and nasty place, and I don't care how tough you are, it will beat you to your knees and keep you there permanently if you let it. You, me, or nobody is gonna hit as hard as life. But it ain't about how hard you hit. It's about how hard you can get it

and keep moving forward. How much you can take and keep moving forward. That's how winning is done! Now if you know what you're worth, then go out and get what you're worth. But you gotta be willing to take the hits and not pointing fingers saying you aint where you wanna be because of him, or her, or anybody! Cowards do that and that ain't you! You're better than that!"

To hell with my depression. Life is a constant comeback. I need to leave behind all anger and regret if I want to live a successful life.

Saturday, February 10, 2007: diary entry

If I really want to be successful, I need to know myself first. I need to be aware of 1) who I am, 2) who I want to be, 3) how I can be that person, and 4) what I want to achieve.

> *1) So, who am I? What are my strengths? I am, I believe, a person who is thoughtful and committed. These principles have helped me reach goals at school and in boxing. Why should I run away from Germany when I know that I can count on my strengths? I can also develop these strengths and reach more goals right here. There is no better place when it comes to being the best version of myself—period!*

But I also need to know my weaknesses and their roots to stop self-sabotaging my life. My biggest weaknesses are probably my fears of being rejected and abandoned. Maybe these fears derive from my childhood. Maybe my parents were overcritical during the first years of my life. Maybe my survival, security, and well-being did depend on them in unhelpful ways when we came to Germany. Maybe I did neglect my needs to make them happy. Today, I still feel over-responsible for my family, often in self-destructive ways. Maybe this feeling was cultivated by my parents' constant fights and depressions. Whatever it was, I should not play the people-pleaser anymore to get acceptance from the outside since it only manifests my fears, my weak boundaries, and my low self-esteem. In addition, I need to change my mind-set. I have almost certainly adopted the attitude of thinking that I'm always the victim. This attitude is wrong and dangerous. It keeps me trapped in blaming others, and it kills my sense of self-competence and self-esteem. If I do not change my mind-set, I will never achieve my dreams.

2) After all these years, I still just want to be a person who is happy and at peace.
3) The critical question is how do I get there with my strengths and weaknesses? I now see that too much thoughtfulness and commitment can be self-destructive, especially when committing to negativity. I'll need to make healthier decisions. I'll need to see and embrace more positive thoughts, emotions, and people. I'll need to repeatedly remind myself that I deserve to be happy, that I am worthy and lovable. If I can make it a habit to think more positively, my emotions will also get more positive. On this journey, it'll help to be around people who don't constantly control me or pull

me down. I'll need to spend more time with encouraging companions when I direct my strengths toward realizing my dreams.

Tackling my weaknesses will not be easy, though. It'll probably be a lifelong struggle. I'll need to repeatedly and compassionately remind myself that I'm an adult now, that my well-being, security, and survival don't depend on anyone anymore, that I can care for myself, and that I am fully responsible for my life. Moreover, if my validation of being worthy and lovable comes from within, I can also change my way of connecting to other people. I can be more optimistic and open. At the same time, conflict with others and saying No is okay and necessary sometimes to protect myself. I need to be more self-supporting to live a life that gives way to happiness and peace.

4) Even though I absolutely wanted to leave Frankfurt, I am once again attracted by this city. Yesterday, I visited Goethe University. They offer fascinating study paths. I'm sure I'll find a program that'll help me develop myself and give back something positive to people.

Monday, April 12, 2007: diary entry

I made a decision. I want to study at Goethe University and become a teacher. I want to study, teach, and discuss the human experience. I want to foster mutual understanding and respect. I want to work with children and teenagers. They're idealistic and not so manipulated by social reality. They are my companions in building a hopefully more happy and peaceful society.

Saturday, October 6, 2007

I received a letter by the Goethe University Frankfurt. I only read the beginning of the first line, "You are accepted ..." With a thankful smile, I put the letter back on the table.

III. Kastel

October 2007-December 2008

"Disturbed communication"

Monday, October 15, 2007

It was my first day at university, and I was excited about starting my new path. I entered Campus Westend through a black metal gate. Looking at the travertine building ahead of me, I crossed a large, green area. Six wings were connected by bent corridors. The facade mixed from yellow to brown. *It made the construction look warm despite its colossal size.*

Impressed, I entered the central, temple-like portico. Many voices resounded in the hall. Students were rushing back and forth. Some were sitting on the stairs to the rotunda. About 37,000 students were enrolled, and I was looking forward to making new friends.

When I took the elevator to the third floor, I spotted a row of wall panels. As I read through them, I learned that the building was built and once owned by the chemical concern Hoechst AG, which produced Zyklon B for the Nazi regime to gas people during World War II. I felt uneasy about this fact and wondered, *Would offering higher education in these rooms today clean this building?*

Friday, December 1, 2007

I went to the student office on Campus Westend. Two graduate students were sitting behind a table. The boy was typewriting; the girl looked up to me. She asked me in English if she could help me. When I responded in German, she opened her eyes widely.

"Sorry, I didn't know you could speak German!" she paused. "Where are you from?"

"I'm from Kastel. I study …," I said.

She interrupted, "I mean, where are you originally from? Are you an exchange student?"

"No," I said, raising my eyebrows and my intonation.

"I just thought. You look like one."

"Really? Why?" I asked. *Was I not dressed "normal," with blue jeans and a pullover?*

"Well, your skin is somewhat brown and your hair is dark," she said.

"But I'm no exchange student. I've lived here for 16 years," I said, trying to control my irritation. *Why did people all the time have to expose and explore my non-whiteness?*

"See! I knew it. So you're not originally German."

"I've got the German passport," I said even though I knew that this was not the answer she was looking for. Yet, I wanted to see how far her "curiosity" would go.

"But not your parents," she insisted.

"They do."

"But at least one of them needs to be not originally from here!" she said.

What an insolence! Tired of her identity game, I said, "My father was born in Iraq."

"See, I knew there was something in you which is not German. I saw it right away!" she said with satisfaction and laughed.

I looked at her, perplexed, and quietly submitted a paper for my professor.

Sunday, December 3, 2007: Diary Entry

I have to go to university tomorrow, but I'm not very motivated. I had thought I would meet educated people there ... If I only knew how to respond to their dull questions. I know I don't look like an "ethnic" German, and I can't and don't want to, either. I am okay as I am. Still, many Germans force me to explain why I, a non-white, live in Germany. Do they think it's their "natural" right as "true" Germans to treat me as a stranger? What is a "true" German? Only someone who is white? I don't want to be forced to explain my identity almost every time I meet someone new. Even some professors play the identity game, stripping me in front of others with their questions. They are stuck in nationalistic and racial thinking. It makes me angry—again. Why do we have a constitution that grants the right to not be discriminated against when I have to experience it again and again? What about my dignity?

My parents have stopped fighting about a divorce. They are now arguing about finances and the houses while I am writing. They don't see that all our properties in Germany are worthless as long as still too many Germans treat us unequally—unjustly. There can be no happiness and no peace without justice. We have houses in Germany, but we are not at home here.

Friday, March 14, 2008: Diary Entry

My membership in my boxing club has become problematic. I skipped training twice for my studies. This evening, I told Tariq that I didn't want to fight anymore and instead focus on my studies. He called me a "loser" and shouted at me in front of everyone, "Then you better never show up again!" Everyone stopped working out. I told him to his face that he didn't care about my future or the future of anyone in our club but only about us stepping in the ring and representing him. He stared at me, surprised that I defended myself. I turned around and left the gym.

My position in the club has become problematic anyway. Most club members are Arabs, Turks, and Russians, in a way strangers in Germany like me. But I'm also becoming an academic now in contrast to most club members. Their reactions on my new path challenge me. Some said, "What? You want to become a teacher? I hated my teachers." Some added that their teachers had prejudices against them and that was why they made their life hell, which made their teachers hate them even more. Some said, "Mashallah! I hope you don't become as arrogant as the students I know." I understand the bitterness they carry inside. I hope I can make a change by following my path and staying friends with them.

Tuesday, April 29, 2008: diary entry

I enjoy my studies. The more knowledge I acquire, the better I can grasp my world. Today, I gave a presentation on family structures in a sociology seminar. I talked about the transition from a dyad (couple-relationship) to a triad (couple with a child). The research I did helped me understand how the communication in my family is disturbed. I've recognized it before, but now I see how it affects *us in our different roles. My mother uses Mamun as a substitute for my father. She always wants him to sit down with her, drink tea, and listen to her stories. Sophia's boyfriends are more than 10 years older than she is. They are another substitute for my father, who has never really recovered from loss of Iraq. All the memories of the past and the news reports about the unending civil war in Iraq pull him down continuously. He has almost no more resources to face our family problems. So, he asks me all the time to solve our problems and convince everyone to change their mind for the sake of peace. But I can't do it any longer—not to the full extent as he wishes. I'm just looking for a relationship outside my family. I want to create my own dyad and triad. I just want to live my life.*

SUNDAY, AUGUST 10, 2008

I started writing a paper on the poverty of Iraqi children. Over the years, I often asked myself how my Iraqi relatives were living. I only had a vague idea from my father's telling. My investigation helped me understand why he wanted us to leave Iraq in 1991. In 1990, Iraq was about to become an industrial state. The mortality rate of children under the age of five was at 5.6 %.[56] When Saddam Hussein illegally invaded Kuwait, the UN Security Council imposed economic sanctions on Iraq. As a result, Iraq lost 90 % of its import and 97 % of its export.[57] Despite their civil use, a 300-page docu-

---

56 David Hilfiker. 2003. Biologische Kriegsführer, in: *IPPNW forum.* 79/03
57 Eric D.K Melby. 1998. Iraq, in: *Economic Sanctions and American Diplomacy,* ed. Haass, Richard N., New York: Council on Foreign Relations Book

ment banned the import of items that had a dual use, which means a potential military use. The list included medicine to treat cancer, X-ray units, laboratory equipment, scientific books, machines for agriculture, spare parts for oil refinery, chemicals to clean water, and much more. The mortality rate of children under age five thus increased more than 200 % within a few months.

When I was a boy in the 1990s, I did not understand the UN sanctions regime. In 2008, I did. *Iraqis were denied their basic needs and, as a result, their value and dignity as human beings.* Due to the lack of clean water, pandemic diseases like cholera and typhus broke out in 1990 after they had been almost eradicated. According to a UN report, 170,000 infants and children under age five died in the first year of the sanctions. Over the next six years, the U.S.A. and the UN Special Commission kept claiming, without solid proof, that Saddam Hussein was hiding weapons of mass destruction while 1.5 million civilians died. Half of them were children under age five according to the UNO.

I also read an article by Hillel Cohen[58], which shocked me with an unbelievable truth. The bombs the U.S.A. dropped in 1991 continued to kill people even long after they had exploded, as if the sudden death from above were not inhumane enough. They contained depleted uranium, which contaminated the groundwater and thus the food chain. As a result,

---

58 Hillel Cohen. 1998. A WEAPON THAT KEEPS KILLING, in: *Challenge to Genozide*, ed. Ramsey Clark. New York: Intl Action Center.

the rate of children suffering from blood cancer shot up over 400 % during the first ten years after the war. Miscarriages and births of dysplastic children exploded in similar numbers.

I was just in the middle of reading another article when my father called me for lunch. I got up and looked at a book that was lying on my desk, "The Children Are Dying."[59] It pictured a young girl who held her head low. Her eyes were hopeless. Her arms looked like sticks. I could count her ribs. I felt terribly sorry for all the children in Iraq. *They were innocent in contrast to most of us. How could we ignore or accept their torturous pains for two decades?*

"Junis, please come now! Stop working!" he shouted again.

We went to Paul-Ehrlich-Straße 4. Mamun and my mother were already sitting at the kitchen table. We sat down. Everyone began eating, except for my mother.

"I can't live like this anymore," she said out of the blue.

"We're all together. We're healthy. What's the problem?" I said.

"I just can't live with this family anymore," she said, got up, and went to the hallway.

I put down my fork and followed her. "What have we done to you?" I asked.

She left the house without a word. I went back to the kitchen.

"Why can she not even look at us?" I asked.

No one responded.

---

[59] Ramsey Clark. 1996. *The Impact of Sanctions on Iraq: The Children Are Dying.* World View Forum Pub

I gulped. Awareness overcame me. *She was right. It could not go on like this anymore.* Mamun played computer games every night and almost all weekend long. Sophia was either drunk or high if she was at home. And my parents usually either yelled at each other or hid, inaccessible, like the rest of us. *I had to free myself from the negativity around me if I wanted to live a successful life.*

Monday, August 11, 2008: diary entry

> When I move out and pay rent for the rest of my studies, I'll toss at least 10,000 Euros out of the window, money that I will never see again. I have saved up 12,000 Euros in my bank account. Last night, I did some research on the internet. I could buy a small studio for around 30,000 Euros in my area. I'll ask my father if he can help me finance it. My plan is to buy a studio and move out by the end of 2008. I need peace to study and to develop myself.

Beginning of December 2008

I found a studio in Liederbach, a small village between Kastel and Frankfurt. My father accompanied me when I met the realtor the first time. On our way back home, he told me that he liked the place, and that he could lend me 10,000 Euros. Astonished by his great support, I thanked him and smiled. *I only had to get together another 8,000 Euros now!*

When we told my mother that we would try to buy that studio, she surprised me as well, "You have 8,000 Euros from your grandmother. She saved up money for all of you. You can use it." I looked at her with big eyes, aware that Oma Erika was one of the greatest people in my life. *She saved me, once again, even though she could not realize it because of her illness.* "Well then, I would very thankfully use it," I said and smiled. *Finally, I could follow my path as a free man.*

IV. Liederbach

January 2009-August 2010

"Something big"

Beginning of January 2009: Diary Entry

I moved into my studio. My father and Asis helped me transport my things from Kastel to Liederbach, the smallest community of the Main-Taunus-Kreis[60]. Liederbach is a rural village with about 8,500 inhabitants. I enjoy the quiet here. I can relax, study, and run cross-country. I live on the fifth floor of a ten-story Plattenbau that was built in 1975.

The building doesn't look very inviting from the outside. The facade of the four towers strung together is clad with brown pebble stones. All windows are positioned in a grid pattern. Each apartment looks like the other from the outside, a dry spectacle across from a Coca-Cola factory with a red cooling tower. The three-story parking lot next to my building is usually completely occupied, but I don't need to worry about that. I can't afford to buy a car anyway.

I pay back 200 Euros a month to my father. Utilities are another 200 Euros. My current income leaves me 10 Euros a week for eating. I have to live very economically, like in 1991 when we came to Germany. My father told me that I don't need to pressure myself with paying off. But I do. It wouldn't be right to owe him so much money and live as if I had all the time in the world to pay the debts. Moreover, owing is a weak, dependent position, which I do not like. The sooner I am debt-free, the sooner I can freely make my own financial decisions. And

---

60 district in the middle of Hesse, part of the Frankfurt/Rhine-Main Metropolitan Region

with all the problems going on in my family, I need to become independent rather soon.

I'm aware that it was risky to finance a studio with no stable work contract. None of my fellow students took such a risk. When they get to know about my housing conditions, they usually look at me with large eyes and ask how I could handle the financial burden in addition to studying. "I have three jobs, and I'm willing to work hard to achieve my goals," I usually tell them. In fact, the first time I saw the studio last November, I already knew I would go for it, no matter what.

Anyway, I'm satisfied with my choice. The building is well maintained. My studio contains 370 square feet. It has new oak laminate flooring, white woodchip wallpaper, a new, white tiled bathroom, and a large balcony with a view to a beautiful, green park. I can even see the Taunus[61] on the horizon. The train station is only a five-minute walk away. I ride to university by train every day. I come home, eat, and study alone. Often, I just eat bread with something before I plunge into my studies. I'm glad I'm finally free to be who I am and to develop myself without constantly having to fight irrational accusations or silent treatment. There are almost no distractions in Liederbach.

Monday, February 2, 2009

IN ADDITION TO WORKING AS a salesman in the MTZ on the weekends and as a tutor and boxing coach at a comprehensive

---

61 a mountain range in Hesse, located north of Frankfurt

school in Hofheim during the week, I started working as a substitute teacher at a grammar school in Frankfurt.

One day, I was supposed to teach a fifth grade in English. When I introduced myself, three girls from the last row immediately started asking me questions. "Where are you from? Are you Turk? Are you Muslim? Do you fast? Do you pray?" I noticed that the three girls were wearing scarves. Their tactlessness annoyed me, and yet I thought I understood their excitement. *I was probably one of the very few teachers who had a visible migration background and with whom they could identify.* I had not noticed any teacher who looked like an immigrant when I walked through the staff room before classes began.

I was on the fence. On the one hand, I did not want to be objectified; I did not want to share parts of my private life in front of a class. On the other hand, I wanted to give these girls something that could encourage them for their future careers.

Before I could comment, however, a boy shouted at the girls, "Shut the fuck up, Aisha!"

"No one of us is called Aisha, you asshole," the girls chorused at once.

I was shocked by the violent language they used. I had thought that diversity would rather be seen as normal among students in an international city like Frankfurt.

With a serious voice, I said to all students, "To make it clear from the beginning, I don't accept discrimination and bullying. You treat each other with respect. You understand?" I sensed that if I had not reacted immediately, it would have been very difficult to establish a socially acceptable, positive working climate afterward. *And if I could not establish such a climate, the students would not learn anything at all.*

Indeed, the class turned quiet at once. I proceeded with the lesson. When I asked the students about their "happiest day during their Christmas vacation," they participated actively. They chose a classmate and listened to what they wanted to share.

Everything worked out as I had planned until I initiated a partner work phase. I walked around and supported each couple with their writing assignment. When I reached the last row where the three girls sat, who absolutely wanted to work together for some reason I had not quite figured out yet, a letter began to make its round behind my back. It reached *Yafet,* a boy in the front. Suddenly, *Sebastian* laughed out loud. "You better check what's going on. They're bullying him again," one of the girls said.

I walked to the front. The class turned dead silent. Yafet was holding his head low. I asked him to show me the letter, which he had just crumpled up. He looked at me, worried and expectant, before he gave me a drawing that showed him with black skin and extra thick, red lips.

I looked at the class with a serious face. "Who drew this?" I asked quietly.

The class remained silent, as if they anticipated what was on the letter.

I waited—until *Lena* asked carefully, "Who drew what?"

"I've got a racist picture here that I'll not show you. But I want to know who drew it."

Still, the class remained quiet. They looked at me with large eyes, almost surprised how much I was determined to not let them get away with it.

"I'll keep the picture with me," I said, looking around. "The one who has drawn it can come to me after the lesson, or meet me in the staff room. I'll wait there for five minutes. If no one shows up, I'll give the picture to your class teacher," I paused and thought about what else to say. I did not want to make too much of the drawing and open Jafet up for additional torments, but I also sensed that the class needed more guidance to create another reality in their classroom. So, I revealed my feelings. "I find it sad how you treat each other. Where is respect and solidarity? You should keep together as one class! This could be one of the best times of your life if you allow it and work together and not against each other."

The students behaved respectfully toward each other after my words. Yet, I had doubts if they fully embraced the sense of community I was trying to make accessible for them. *I was just a random substitute teacher who had no regular contact with them.*

BEGINNING OF JUNE 2009: DIARY ENTRY

I've got a financial problem. My expenses exceed my income. But I do not want to stop paying off the apartment. My work as a substitute teacher does not bring regular income. In May, it brought only 100 Euros. The school did not need more substitutes. I need to look for a job that brings regular income.

Wednesday, July 1, 2009

I watched the news, "The pregnant 31-year-old Egyptian Marwa Alim El-Sherbini was stabbed 18 times during a trial in a Dresdener court by an ethnic German immigrant from Russia. Marwa testified in a case of verbal abuse. Her 3-year-old child had to watch the murderous act. When her husband ran to rescue her, he was shot by a police officer who mistook him for the attacker. The motive of the 28-year-old murderer was hate against foreigners and against Islam."

Even though I was shocked, and even though I felt deeply sorry for *Marwa* and her family, the news report did not surprise me on second thought. *The restraining threshold from racist thoughts to violent deeds is small,* I knew from my experiences as a young boy—first it is degrading thoughts, then suspicious eyes, bullying, insults, persecution, and punches. In Marwa's case, unfortunately, it was even a killing knife.

Still, many German politicians systematically played down the problem in the mainstream media, calling the murder "an islamophobic individual case" even though lethal attacks against "Middle-Eastern-looking" people had a long history in Germany.

The case of Marwa caused me to ponder. *Why did many politicians divert the public and talk about security problems at a particular court without discussing the cause of this personal tragedy—racism, nationalism, and Islamophobia? Why did they not focus on Marwa's claims? Was it because they were part of the establishment and part of the problem? Was it because power politics largely defined itself, not through its agenda, but by what is not on the agenda?*

I pondered for a long time. *What could we do to transform our society from divisiveness, hate, and violence to more connectedness, happiness, and peace. What could I do beyond teaching in my everyday life?*

Tuesday, August 6, 2009: diary entry

My mother asked me if I was interested in going to Italy. I said, "Yes!" I hope we can improve our relationship. I know that she loves the beach. I love it as well.

Since I have moved out, the tension between us has decreased. We don't fight that much anymore. Sometimes, distance helps heal relationships. Yet, healing takes more than that. Forgiveness, good will, and constant effort are necessary as well. I visit my parents once a week, and I try to avoid the critical talking points: religion, culture, politics, money, and properties. I want to build up trust by focusing on the things we have in common and enjoy. My father will go to Italy as well. The last time we went together on vacation was in June 2004—before I met Ceylin. Too long ago!

Sunday, October 11, 2009: diary entry

We had a beautiful time in Italy, like back in the 1990s. We enjoyed the warm weather. We walked on the beach. We swam together in the ocean. We ate ice cream almost every night.

We also spent an entire day walking in the small valleys in our beloved Venice. We had a happy and peaceful time together, alhamdulillah!

Before we went to Italy, I had applied for two scholarships—HORIZON and FULBRIGHT. I spotted the first Horizon poster when I walked along a corridor in the IG Farben building (Campus Westend). The poster pictured three fine-dressed students: a lightly tanned guy with black hair, an Asian girl with black hair, and another lightly tanned girl with black hair. Their looks attracted me subconsciously. I read the text, "Did you choose teacher training? Are you a teacher trainee? Did you or your parents migrate to Germany? Today 33 % of the pupils but only 1 % of the teachers in German schools have a migration background. The Horizon Scholarship financially and ideationally supports outstanding prospective teachers who have a migration background." Horizon seemed to be looking for someone like me, I thought. Without a doubt, I needed the money. So, I applied.

This week, I received a positive answer to my application. From November on, I'll be a Horizon scholar and get 650 Euros per month over two years. End of financial crisis, alhamdulillah! 250 students applied in Berlin, Hamburg, and Frankfurt for the scholarship. 11 people were accepted in Berlin, nine in Hamburg, and only three in Frankfurt. I was successful.

On top, my mother surprised me again. She said she was proud of me and that she bought me a car for 600 Euros, a 1991 black VW Golf GT Special. I love it. It belonged to the owner of the gas station in the MTZ, where my father used to work before he got *cancer. I thanked my mother with a big hug. I am happy that I am on good terms with her again.*

Tomorrow, the winter term will start. I'm relaxed. I know I can manage university.

MID-OCTOBER 2009

In January 2005, heartbreak and cognitive dissonance due to the gaps I had experienced between the theory and the human practices of Islam made me drift away from physical religious practices. *Many alleged Islamic rules were not religious,* I saw, *but rather cultural and political and thus crippled by the human greed for power.* I did not pray on a regular basis anymore. I did not fast, either. I drifted toward spiritual practices, pondering the meaning of our existence, sometimes talking to Allah in silence, and trying to understand truths that went beyond our physical existence. I still had faith in a higher power. I was still enchanted by the 99 names of Allah, especially by those that expressed the face of love: beneficent, providing, gentle and kind, grateful, watchful, responsive, steadfast, merciful, and repeatedly forgiving. Principles, I knew, I could with all my imperfections never fully live up to but still wanted to strive after to improve my relationships with others, with Allah, and with myself on my quest for happiness and peace. Moreover, I repeatedly reminded myself of the two Islamic virtues, sabur (patience and endurance) and shukr (thankfulness), which would make my imperfect journey more bearable. And when relationships improved or dreams became reality, I thanked Allah from my inmost soul.

I thanked Allah all the time, actually, for providing my basic needs: food, clean water, fresh air, a calm walk in the forest, a warm bed to sleep in, and much more.

Wednesday, October 21, 2009: diary entry

I'll take my TOEFL exam for my Fulbright application on Friday, but I haven't prepared yet. I'm worried about Oma Erika. She has been diagnosed with esophageal cancer. I visited her in the hospital last weekend after she had undergone surgery. In a couple of days, the doctors will begin the radiation treatment. I pray she becomes healthy again.

Next Monday, I'll participate in the final assessment at the Fulbright center in Berlin. I have already successfully competed against all the applicants at Goethe University. If I am successful in Berlin, one of my long-time dreams will come true.

Saturday, November 14, 2009: diary entry

Today is a good day. Today is probably the greatest day in my life. After I came home from university, I opened my mailbox and found a blue letter from Berlin. I opened it and only read *the first line. I jumped into the air with the brightest smile! What a life! I am so blessed. I am nominated by the Berlin Fulbright Commission for a nine-month scholarship, including up to $ 30,400 USD, alhamdulillah! In August 2010, I will go to the U.S.A.! The land of liberty and of the pursuit of happiness! Dreams become true in 2010!*

Thursday, December 17, 2009: diary entry

It was around noon. I was listening to a lecture on macroeconomics when I received the text message from my father, "Your mother and I will go to your grandmother now. She's not doing well." I left the lecture hall right away to call him. He told me to stay in Frankfurt and call him later. When I called him in the afternoon, he told me that Oma Erika had died.

Tears are filling my eyes while I'm writing. I already miss her so much. She took care of us in every sense. I always felt her love. Even when she was so ill, she would call me with a warm voice, "My dear." Oma Erika, may you rest in peace. I love you.

Beginning of August 2010

When the summer term ended, I went to Onkel Walter to say goodbye before my departure to the U.S.A. Even though our families did not keep in close contact after the dispute over Paul-Ehrlich-Straße 4 in 1997, I thought it would be appropriate to visit him since we still invited each other for milestone birthdays. *Going to the U.S.A. would be just as special,* I thought.

We were sitting in his living room, opposite each other, when he asked me, "How did you get this scholarship? Was it your migration background again?"

His question made me recollect how my English professor had opened her eyes widely when I told her that I had qualified for a Fulbright scholarship. She said the number of applicants had decreased and that it would be easier to get a scholarship these days. I wondered, *What did envy offer people except for burdening relationships?*

Controlled, I said to Onkel Walter, "No, it was not my background. My grades were excellent. Further, I ran through various assessments and convinced the committee with my knowledge and with my personality. Actually, the same procedure applied for the Horizon scholarship."

He looked at me with a raised eyebrow, "So how exactly did you convince them?"

"I guess by my knowledge of the U.S.A. and my intercultural competencies."

"Was the competition tough?"

"Well, principally every student of all German universities was able to apply. In the end, only six students received a nine-month full scholarship for university-level studies."

"You're lucky. You're given an exceptional opportunity. Congratulations."

"Thank you," I said, smiling friendly and knowing that I was not lucky. *I had started from almost zero in 1991, and I achieved something big.*

V. Fullerton

August 2010-April 2011

"Peaceful rise"

Friday, August 6, 2010

I LANDED AT LOS ANGELES around noon, after an 11-hour flight. Even though I lacked sleep, I got up from my seat with energy and full of hope. *U.S.A., the nation of immigrants, as they say.* With a bright smile, I thanked the flight attendants and followed the passengers inside the building. We lined up at a counter. When it was my turn, I showed my passport. "Wait a minute, Sir. Something showed up here. We need to check you," the officer said. He dialed a number and told the person on the line nothing more than my name. Next, he asked me to wait offside. The passengers behind me were allowed to enter. I began to feel nervous. *Something was wrong,* I sensed. I had never had any problems with flying in Europe.

After a while, two officers in black uniforms came and asked me to walk with them. When I read their tags, "Homeland Security," I understood what was going on. They represented the institution that was installed under George W. Bush after 9/11 to protect the U.S.A. from terrorists. I had not expected they would examine me, too. Walking between the officers, I briefly looked over my shoulder. The remaining passengers at the desk stared at me while I was led off like a criminal. I felt harassed. *What an embarrassing beginning.*

I entered a small interrogation room, which had no window. The young officer sat down behind a large table. "Take a seat. Your documents, please," he said in a serious tone. He looked at them for a couple of minutes before he started asking me questions: "Who are you? Where are you from? Where were you born? Who are your parents? What are they doing? Where were they born? Have you ever been in the U.S.A.? Do you have contacts in the U.S.A.? What are you planning to do here? Where? Why in the U.S.A.? Do you have a religious background? Knowledge in chemistry? Do you plan a terrorist attack? Are you telling the truth?" The interrogation took 15 minutes. I answered all questions as calmly as I could even though I was quite worried I could say a word or behave in a way that might get me into trouble. *I had nothing to hide,* I knew, *and yet it depended on his assessment of my behavior whether I should be considered a threat to the public and sent back or whether I should be allowed to enter the country.*

"You know why we ask you all these questions?" he said.

"I guess because I possess the Iraqi passport as well," I said even though I had never travelled with my Iraqi passport since my naturalization in 1991.

"Correct. Your country and your name are on the black list," he said and looked deeply into my eyes.

We had reached the critical part of the interrogation. Either he would believe what I had said—or not. Then what? Did he believe that I was a terrorist? I had no idea how I was supposed to respond. I just firmly kept eye contact with him.

After a tense moment, he said, "But you're okay. Enjoy your time at California State University, Fullerton. I've heard they like partying there. Welcome to America!"

"Thank you," I said, relieved that he would finally let me go.

We got up and shook hands. It felt odd. I did not take the interrogation personally. I knew *the officer was required per law to target me.* Nonetheless, it did not assuage the stress I felt.

After I had gone through customs, I went outside. Many people were bustling about on the curb. Some were picked up by family. Some caught a taxi. I located a person who wore a blue T-shirt. She put me on the list for a "Super-Shuttle." The international office of CSUF had recommended this shuttle service. Shortly, a blue Ford van stopped by.

I sat down at the rear seat. After five other passengers had been added, the driver hit the road. He turned up the volume of his radio a little bit. A famous saxophonist, who I did not know, was announced. Smooth jazz music began to play. It relaxed my mind. Through the window, I looked at my new world. Cars and streets were wider than in Europe. Along the freeway, I saw trimmed palm trees peacefully rising from the horizon into the light blue sky. *What a beautiful sight!* I thought and smiled. Every now and then, my eyelids dropped. I was jet-lagged, but my curiosity always made me open my eyes again. I felt like I was in a trance.

After more than an hour driving and dropping off passengers, we arrived in Fullerton. I tipped the driver 20 %, as I had been advised. "Thank you, brother," he said. "You're welcome, brother," I replied, surprised about his words. *No driver had ever called me brother in Germany.* We smiled at each other before we continued our separate journeys.

I waited with my baggage in front of the Fullerton Marriot Hotel. Across the street, a display showed 101 degrees Fahrenheit. I had no idea how many degree Celsius that was, but it certainly felt like more than 30 degrees Celsius. The hot air warmed me up immediately. *This was my kind of weather!* In all those years in Germany, I did not get used to its weather. Too many months, it stayed cloudy, gray, and chilly. Lasting cloud covers were almost normal. Even in summer, I quite often could not see the sun. Now, I was looking at the golden star gloriously shining. *Blue sky and sunlight, what a great delight!* My face shined.

To the right, I beheld the campus of CSUF. Students were walking on a smooth, pre-fabricated pathway that meandered through a neatly cut lawn. The grass blades were thicker than in Germany. They had to store more water due to the heat, like in Mosul. *Fullerton and Mosul almost lay on the same latitude,* I knew from my travel planning. Both places had a high number of sunny, dry days over the year. While the students walked in the sunshine, I looked at the trimmed palm trees that grandly rose into the sky. Even though I could not name the sorts of the trees, they sweetly reminded me of my childhood in Iraq. Next to the trees, I spotted a beautiful, marble fountain in front of a white, flat-roofed building. Six floors seemed to hide behind the unusual, slit-like windows.

Suddenly, someone called me from behind. I turned around and saw a middle-aged, clean-shaven man, smiling.

"Tom?" I asked, smiling back.

"Yay, I found you. Welcome to America, my friend!" he said.

We shook hands, smiling nonstop. I was excited to meet my temporary host father. Tom wore a nice dress shirt and suit pants. His hair was short and brown. He was my height, a bit overweight, and his big, brown eyes told me that he was glad to meet me. I felt warmly welcomed.

"Let's get in the car. I'll take you to your new home, to Yorba Linda," he said.

While we drove through Yorba Linda, I spotted large residential lots. Many properties were not enclosed by fences or walls like in Germany. Instead, I beheld open, manicured gardens with flowers and palm trees. Some properties contained a swimming pool. In other areas, horse trails went along the streets. Time and again, people were riding next to us.

"What a beautiful place to live!" I said.

"Oh, you like it. That's good to hear," he said and laughed.

Tom seemed to be a fun-loving person. I easily took a shine to him.

As we kept driving, we began to talk about our families. I sensed that he was a family man, like me. He told me, with shiny eyes, how excited everyone was to meet me. I was at least as much excited to meet them. Tom had sent me a picture of his young family before my departure.

After our ten-minute drive, I could see them in person. His family was awaiting us on the lawn in front of their huge, light brown house, which had a sloping roof. We got out of the car and met the family half way. We were all smiling. *Janel,* his wife, gave me a warm hug. Next, their three children hugged me as well. Christine was 6, John 3, and Cathy 1 year old. *They were my new family.* I counted myself lucky.

Mid-August 2010

Tom's family also hosted another student from Germany, *Emmanuel.* He came from Herrenberg, in the south of Germany, and arrived one day after me. Tom's family did not volunteer in the "seven-day homestay program" that year because they were busy attending to their baby, Cathy. But since no family had consented to host Emmanuel and me, the program supervisor had contacted Tom two days before my arrival. They agreed to host us right away. I was amazed by their readiness to help and welcome us with open arms.

When Emmanuel and I met in the living room for the first time, we briefly examined each other. "Hi," we said. *Staying together would only be for some days. Emmanuel seemed to think the same.* We had come all the way to primarily meet the people of the U.S.A.

Our initial chilly greetings thawed within a few days as we became closer and integrated into the family. We easily played with Christine and John, and we often fed Cathy in her baby high chair when we all sat down to eat. Almost every day, Janel cooked for us, and we would help her. Janel was what many Americans called "Korean-American." One day, we helped her prepare kimchi, a traditional Korean food. We chopped cabbage and cut garlic, chives, and an onion while she prepared a special sauce. On another day, we helped Tom prepare a U.S. barbecue. We seasoned juicy steaks and plenty of vegetables and put them on the grill in their backyard after we had done some yard work together. In addition to all the activities at home, Tom or Janel drove us around whenever it was possible. They took us to our campus, so that we could explore it. They drove us to malls and helped us choose cell phone providers. We also went with the entire family to Downtown Disney District, to Legoland, to Fashion Island, and to the beautiful beaches of Orange County (OC). They paid for everything all the time without ever talking about money. Instead, they explained to us how things worked in the U.S.A.: for instance getting a driver's license or health care. Similarly, they were eager to learn how things worked in Germany. After our talks in the evening, the kids always kissed us goodnight. Sometimes, Emmanuel or I read a bedtime story to them before we, the adults, met in the spacious living room. Tom, Janel, Emmanuel, and I would sit on a pillowy coach, snack, talk, and laugh time and again. I was fascinated by the love we received. *Emmanuel and I became a part of the family.*

When Tom drove Emmanuel and me around during the day, he often received calls from vendors. Still, it did not prevent him from showing us OC. Sometimes, he stopped at his favorite cafes and bought us coffee and bagels. *Being with Tom was like a present.*

During our drives, I often spotted oil wells even in the middle of neighborhoods. It made me ponder. *In Germany, state regulations or citizens' movements would probably have prohibited the inclusion of an industrial area in a residential area for health and security reasons.*

The oil wells also reminded me of the war in 2003. *If the U.S.A. drilled their own oil without visible restrictions, why then did they invade Iraq in 2003? Was it really the insatiable greed for oil of a developed economy that had to go beyond national borders to grow further? Or was it the political struggle for a new U.S. world order? Or perhaps it was both? A win-win situation?*

One day, I asked Tom how much oil the U.S.A. produced. He said, "Almost half of what we consume. The bigger half is imported from countries like Canada, Venezuela, and Iraq." At that moment, I told him that my father was born in Iraq. Without delay, he said, "I'm sorry for what happened. The U.S.A. had no good reason to invade Iraq. It's a catastrophe for the people." I appreciated his empathy.

My studies in Germany helped me analyze politics by investigating various categories: the conflict situation, involved parties, interests, power, and efficient and legitimate solutions. In the U.S.A., I rediscovered an unresolved problem. Tom was a committed Republican and a Christian. He believed in the Christian command "to love your neighbor as yourself." And even though he voted for George W. Bush as president in 2000, he condemned the destructive U.S. foreign policies that followed 9/11. *The legitimacy of political power was questionable, even in a democracy, and especially in the international arena,* I noticed as strongly as never before.

That day, I also pondered over the world politics once again. *Has the time not come to prevent Machiavellian wars? Has the time not come to create a more just "world order"? Has the time not come to make the UN Security Council more legitimate? Has the time not come to add as many legitimate states as possible to the Security Council? Has the time not come to unanimously put the right to life and the dignity of human beings first when we face questions of international peace?*

Friday, August 20, 2010

Even though Emmanuel and I enjoyed our time together with our host family, we looked for separate dwellings. We wanted to live with U.S. Americans and enhance our cultural horizon and our English language skills. Since we could not find anything workable and affordable in seven days, however, Tom and Janel invited us to stay as long as we wanted. We thanked them and smiled. I was touched by their hospitality and impressed by their unconditional support.

Orientation Week began on August 16. At the end of the week, all international students were invited to the home of the president of CSUF. I was sitting next to Emmanuel with hundreds of students in a white tent that was put up in the president's huge backyard. In his speech, the president welcomed everyone before he proudly announced that three international Fulbright students were enrolled at CSUF that term. Next, he called my name and asked me to stand up. I could hardly believe what was happening. When I got up, everyone applauded for a long moment. *I was treated with extra respect for my achievement.* I felt very much honored.

After dinner, a picture was taken of us three Fulbrighters with the president, who stood in the center and laid his hand on my shoulder. I smiled widely, embracing the myth: *U.S.A., the land of opportunity.* Tom was present as well. He stood behind the photographer and told the international student supervisor next to him how lucky he felt to host me.

After the photo shoot, Tom approached me. He put his hand on my shoulder and said, "I've hosted lots of students throughout the years, but never a Fulbrighter. I have respect for you. Not only because for what you've achieved, but because I can tell that you're a very thoughtful person." He touched me with his words. I felt appreciated. "Thank you, Tom," I said, "And you are a very loving person, I can tell."

Saturday, August 21, 2010

Since Emmanuel and I did not find separate dwellings, we decided to share an apartment in a residence across from CSUF. After we had moved into our one bedroom apartment, he bought us beer and chips from the supermarket close by. *One beer would not be too bad,* I thought. Yet, it was the first alcoholic drink for me in years. We were sitting on the beige, fluffy carpet in the living room, watching a movie on his Mac Book, when I began to feel dizzy. Emmanuel noticed it. As I weaved to the kitchen, he followed me, grabbed my shoulders, and laughed out so loud, like he often did, that I began to laugh as well. *What a hilarious guy.* We were building a friendship. I was glad to live with Emmanuel.

Sunday, September 19, 2010

Tom invited Emmanuel and me for a barbecue. He called me and asked what I wanted to eat. I told him that I ate just about everything, except pork.

Even though I had distanced myself from physical religious rules, I kept avoiding pork. My stomach did not tolerate it anymore. Besides, pork was usually not the healthiest meat anyway, I knew.

Tom answered easily, "Okay, good, I'll take care of that!" *Pork or no pork was not a big deal for Tom,* I noticed gladly, remembering how my mother often complained that she could not eat pork because she felt bad about doing it since my father and I were Muslims. Even though I repeatedly told her that she could eat whatever she wanted as far as I was concerned, she always hid somewhere where no one could see her when she ate pork. I always felt sorry for her. *She should have been with us.* Nevertheless, I also had difficulties understanding her. *She could just have sat with us and tolerated that some people don't eat pork.*

At least, Tom, his family, and Emmanuel were open. Tom picked us up, and we had a delicious pork-free and pork-rich barbecue. We were sitting at their round table on their terrace in the backyard. As we did every time, we first held our hands and praised and thanked God for the food before we began to eat. I enjoyed our ritual. It reminded me of the prayer my father used to speak in Arabic before we would break the fast in Ramadan. I felt very connected to Tom's family and to Emmanuel.

SATURDAY, OCTOBER 16, 2010

I was sitting at my desk, eating cereal and watching the German news on my laptop. The German chancellor, Angela Merkel, was speaking to young members of the Christian Democratic Union. She said, "Of course the multi-cultural approach, the idea of people with different cultural backgrounds living happily side by side, has utterly failed in Germany." While talking, she nodded vehemently and moved her hand. Disgusted, I swallowed the cereal in my mouth. Never before had I seen such a committed performance by her and such an excited audience.

She continued, "It's not acceptable that twice as many of them (immigrants) don't graduate from school. It's not acceptable that twice as many of them don't have an associate degree. This is causing our social problems of the future, and this is why integration is so important, and this means, in the first place, that those who want to live in our society do not only have to abide to our laws, but they have to, above all, learn our language."

I shut down my laptop and walked to the mirror on my wardrobe. My pulse shot up. I felt angry. *Ms. Merkel, what about the years-long lack of German language courses for immigrants? What about the German education system that selects and allocates children chiefly based on their German skills when they are only 10 years old? Do you really believe immigrants fail at school because they don't want to learn German? Have you not seen the results of the PISA[62] studies? Why do you ignore that the German education system belongs to the few in the world that*

---

[62] Programme for International Student Assessment is a worldwide study by the Organisation for Economic Co-operation and Development (OECD)

have severely disadvantaged immigrants? How can you blame those who you fail to serve for the failure of your system? Why don't you finally reform the German education system? And what about the hard-working immigrants who prevailed in your system? Is it coincidence that you left them out when inciting the people? What kind of worldview do you have? Or do you "only" intend to catch right-wing voters for the next election? Do you feel strongly with the majority of Germans voting for your cheap propaganda? What about the constitutional promise of freedom, equality, and human rights? What about the right to not be discriminated against because of one's language? Do you know how much your immigrant-baiting damaged social cohesion in Germany today? Can you take the responsibility for the future consequences?

After a moment of indignation, I became aware of how lucky I was to live in the U.S.A. *In contrast to Ms. Merkel and mainstream Germany, Mr. Obama[63] and mainstream U.S.A. acknowledged and valued that they were a nation of immigrants.*

I full-heartedly embraced how diversity was lived at CSUF. I attended three evening classes with about 20 students in each class. We had different skin colors, dialects, ages, work experiences, religious beliefs, political views, and relationship statuses. Everyone accepted it as a matter of course. No one was asked where he or she "originally came from." No one was stripped because of his or her appearance. *We were all the same—just students.*

---

63 Barack Hussein Obama II, served as the 44th President of the United States from 2009 to 2017

I developed more contacts in the first three weeks than in three years of studying in Frankfurt. My classmates and I called each other regularly. We met in groups in cafes to do our homework. We chatted, read, philosophized, and laughed together. When we had questions, we contacted our professors, who were always helpful. They would quickly reply to our e-mails and invite us to their office. They were glad about our interest and often equipped us with more resources. After our discussion in our evening classes, my friends and I sometimes spontaneously had a drink somewhere. We also met for the cinema just two weeks after classes had started. I usually wore a T-shirt when we were together. None of them stared at my scars or asked what happened, like at Goethe University. We just enjoyed our time. I felt like a normal human being. *Studying at CSUF was much richer than at Goethe University;* it was developing one's life to the fullest while connecting with others without unnecessary complications.

Sunday, October 31, 2010

I also had many international friends. Some came for their studies from Japan or the Philippines, others from Greece, Mexico, and France. In addition to Emmanuel, I befriended more students from Germany, mostly from Tübingen University. We often had lots of fun together.

On Halloween, we all headed to Isla Vista to join a street party that attracted thousands of students every year. We drove with three cars. I picked up Christina, Natalie, and Cornelia in the morning with my green 1999 model VW Golf convertible.

I had bought the car at the beginning of October since public transportation was insufficient compared to Frankfurt. It took 90 minutes, for instance, to get from our apartment to the beach by bus, while it was a 30-minute ride by car.

The warm sun was shining brightly while we were driving on the 101 along the Pacific coast. Fresh ocean air was blowing in our faces. *It was the perfect weather: not chilly, not too hot.* Countless waves washed along the sandy beach that was stretching for miles in front of the dark blue ocean while palm trees popped into our view—*creating a fantastic dream.* Christina, sitting next to me, and Natalie and Cornelia, sitting on the rear seats, were singing along with *Katy Perry's*[64] "Teenage Dream." Time and again, we stopped and took photos of each other, posing and laughing in front of my car with the ocean in the background. *I was experiencing the car ride of my life!*

In Isla Vista, we danced and sang all night long. I felt as happy and free as never before.

Beginning of November 2010
Life was colorful. Life was cultivating. Life was vibrant at CSUF.
Even though my schedule was packed with assignments, I was

---

[64] born 10/25/1984, American singer and songwriter

eager to enrich my campus experience as much as possible. After classes had begun, I became a member of a campus association, the Middle Eastern Student Society. Most members had a Middle Eastern background. We largely communicated in English and soon all became friends. In November, we organized an information day on campus. On posters and flip charts, we presented our countries of origin and other topics, such as "Arabs in the U.S.A." and the "Palestine conflict." We also provided Arabic food and music. Hundreds of students joined and enjoyed our event. In the afternoon, we were all dancing together to belly dance music. I was thrilled. *Never before had I gotten the chance to celebrate my heritage in "the West" so freely.*

Thursday, November 11, 2010

Emmanuel and I were often invited by Tom's family to join them going to church on Sundays. On Thanksgiving Day, we all went to the evening dinner their church had organized. We were served typical American food: turkey with cranberry sauce, yams, and pumpkin cake for dessert. I was enjoying another part of American culture, which I had only seen in the movies by then.

Paul, Tom's middle-aged friend, who had asked me in church two weeks earlier if I was a Christian, was present, too. I had told him that I was a Muslim to make things easier since I assumed that my identity was relatively complex. When I lined up at the buffet, he handed me a book,

" 'Inside the Revolution.' It says that Islam isn't the answer, and that not Jihad but Jesus is the way." I was stunned. *Did he think he was morally superior because he was Christian?* Tom intervened immediately, "Paul, this is just a book written by someone. Everyone can believe what he or she wants." "Sure," Paul said and disappeared. For a moment, I felt lost. *Why did people use religion to classify people they did not even know as wrong and inferior?* Tom must have seen it in my eyes. He put his hand on my shoulder. "Don't take his insensitivity personally. I like you," he said.

Tom was my hero. He protected me from Paul's selfishness and from my self-pitying. He calmed me down with sympathy, and he made me smile with a compliment. *We needed more Toms in this world.*

End of March 2011

I hardly noticed how fast time went by while I was studying, thriving, running, celebrating, traveling, and discovering California with my friends.

At the end of February, I flew to New Orleans to participate in a four-day Fulbright enrichment seminar that had the title "Greening of the Planet: Global Challenges, Local Solutions." I worked together with Fulbright students from all over the world. It was an incredibly empowering experience to see how we, without really knowing each other, could create and develop ideas together that could help all humanity.

Four weeks before my final exams at CSUF, the reality of my return journey became inescapable, however, and it troubled me more than I had expected.

Sunday, March 27, 2011: diary entry

It's 4 a.m., and I can't sleep. I was just standing at the end of the long corridor that leads to room G25: Emmanuel's and my apartment. I was gripping the stair rail, looking at the city in front of me, and pondering for one hour ... Orange clouds are running away from light pollution. Heavy thoughts encircle my mind. Why can't I hop on and escape reality? Why am I who I am? Ungraspable emotions pull me down from deep inside ... Tonight, I pulled out many cigarettes. It has been years since I smoked, and I still feel dizzy. My hands are trembling ... but I need to write. The sound of spitting tobacco was drowned out by the far-away horn of Amtrak[65]. Soon, I'll have to go back to Germany. Then WHAT? I thought distance would help me forget. It didn't, though. All at once, it feels as if my old traumas have become alive again. My family, Marcus, Ceylin, and all the places and scars inside of me. Ya Allah, what crime have I permitted to be haunted by those demons? I am tired of being myself. I DON'T WANT TO GO BACK TO GERMANY!

---

65 passenger railroad service that provides medium- and long-distance intercity service in the contiguous United States

Saturday, April 23, 2011

My friends and I went to the Exchange Club in Los Angeles on my last day in the U.S.A. We danced the entire night on the huge dance floor. Green lights shot from the tall black dome into the dancing masses while the DJ played electronic beats. Around 1 a.m., Emmanuel and I walked down the stairs behind the dance floor. We went outside to a small, fenced-in area next to a backstreet. We smoked a cigarette and looked at each other.

Suddenly, Emmanuel broke the silence. "I'm gonna miss you man."

"I'm gonna miss you, too. One year together. Best time of my life."

"Are you ready to go home?"

"I don't know," I paused. "I miss my family. But I rather feel like staying here."

"Okay, stop! Otherwise, I will start to cry. You shouldn't leave now. I will visit you in Germany when I come next month. Let's go and celebrate, my friend."

I smiled even though I, all of a sudden, felt dizzy. I hardly managed to follow Emmanuel upstairs. When I reached the dance floor, my friends looked at me with concerned faces. "Dude, are you okay? You're pale. You're sweating. Sit down! We'll get you a water," they said. I sat down on the floor in front of the bar for 15 minutes, too weak to get up.

Jennifer, Emmanuel's girlfriend, who was visiting us from Germany, sat next to me. She saw it in my eyes. "It's the stress.

You've been here for almost one year. Now you suddenly realize that you will leave everything behind and go back. I went through it last year when I studied in Niagara Falls. I didn't want to leave, either. Don't worry! You'll manage!" she said.

"You're probably right," I said. "I guess many things will be pretty much the same when I go back—except me. I have changed. I felt so good in the United States," I paused. "I met so many kind and open people. I had so much joy and freedom."

"Don't worry! You'll manage!" she said and smiled.

I smiled back, hoping that she was right and yet knowing that life would never be the same again when I go back. Compared to Germany, the prejudices I faced in the U.S.A. were very rare. Instead, I received lots of love. Wistful, I got up to enjoy my last few hours in the U.S.A.

After we had danced for the rest of the night, my friends dropped me off at LAX[66]. In the gray of dawn, when the sun began to rise, we said "Goodybe" to each other with a long embrace.

---

66 Los Angeles International Airport

VI. Kastel

April 2011-May 2011

"Ius sanguinis"

Saturday, April 23, 2011

After I had gone through customs at Frankfurt International Airport, I spotted Mamun standing in the arrival hall in a crowd of people. We both smiled at each other and met half way. He gave me a soft handshake. I hugged him and kissed his cheeks.

"Hey, brother! Good to see you again. How are you?"

"I'm good, thanks. And you?" he asked.

"Thanks, I'm good," I said. "Did you come alone?"

"Yes. Baba flew to Iraq a few days ago. Mama is at home. She's tired."

"Oh really?" I was surprised about my father's departure. "How come he suddenly went to Iraq? He e-mailed me two weeks ago that he couldn't wait to see me and pick me up at the airport."

"I don't know," he said, indifferently.

I was alarmed. I knew *this* kind of indifference. As a rule, Mamun tried to keep out of family problems. *Did my parents fight again?*

While he led me to his car, more questions came to my mind. *What happened during the time I was away? Could I continue from where I left in 2010? Or would unforeseen challenges await me?* Uncertainty gradually diminished my happiness to see my family again. Even though we skyped regularly when I lived in Fullerton, I reckoned that they might have withheld some problems from me, *probably because I was too far away and unable to help on the ground.*

After a 15-minute drive, we arrived in Kastel. We entered Frankfurter Weg 7. "Hello, I'm back," I called out and waited—but no one responded. Mamun went upstairs to the bathroom. I dropped my baggage on the floor, wondering, *Where was my mother?*

I stepped inside the kitchen, where I spotted a book on the table, "The Great Cover Up. For Integration, against Islamism," by Alice Schwarzer, a popular German feminist, who had published many texts on that topic. I felt weary. *Another source that fed my mother's negative thoughts and feelings about Islam?* Disheartened, I opened the book.

As I skimmed through the text, I recollected the book review, which I had read in Fullerton. According to Ms. Schwarzer, the integration of immigrants failed because Germany applied the wrong kind of tolerance: an uncritical sympathy for all foreigners, motivated by the history of Nazi-Germany. Ms. Schwarzer thus celebrated the 2009 court ruling, which revoked the possibility of exemption from coeducational swimming lessons for Muslim girls, as a victory for good and hard-fought Western democracy against the alleged evil Islamism that contaminated Germany. *As if there were only ONE political Islam, and as if the majority of German Muslims followed this antidemocratic political Islam, and as if the 2009 ruling made the German society more just, peaceful, and happy again.*

Pictures flashed through my mind: I entered the staff room of the Frankfurter grammar school where I used to work. A teacher put an article on the wall and proudly proclaimed, "The Higher Administrative Court of Münster forces female Muslim students to participate in swimming classes. They can wear a burkini if they wish. The ruling is just and legitimate." Three teachers rejoiced with mischievous comments, "Now their stinky parents can complain as much as they want." "Thank God the law is on our side." "Finally our Aishas have to swim with boys." I was perplexed and wondered, *Did the three teachers really feel better after expressing their hatred against conservative Muslims? And what did the silent teachers in the staff room think?*

I put down the book and took a deep breath, aware that I needed to calm down.

Pensive, I looked outside the window at the Park & Ride where Ceylin and I used to meet. *Was she all right? What was she doing? Where did she live?* I took another deep breath, filled with old regret—*Ceylin.*

Suddenly, my mother entered the kitchen. She said "Hello."

I turned around, said "Hello," and smiled even though her look almost frightened me. Her face was swollen. Her eyes were tired.

We kissed each other's cheeks.

"How are you?" I asked, watchfully.

"I'm okay," she said in a low voice.

She wasn't. She had dark rings. "When does Baba come back?" I asked, cautiously.

"I don't know." She raised her shoulders.

I hesitated, but I could not hold back the question, "Did you quarrel again?"

"It had been difficult with him while you were in America."

"Why? What happened?"

"He talked about money and properties all the time, and I don't want to talk about it." *What properties, and why now?* I wondered, but I did not ask. I did not want to bother her with more unpleasant questions. In addition, I knew, *Sooner or later, I would be confronted with it anyway.*

END OF APRIL 2011

My mother and Mamun moved in Frankfurter Weg 7 after Oma Erika had died. Even though it was not usual for us to discuss financial matters, I knew that my parents' pension did not sufficed for a living. I had thus set my hand to task and pushed my parents to rent out Paul-Ehrlich-Straße 4 before I went to Fullerton. I advertised it on the internet and also helped empty and clean the house. We had many potential renters and agreed to rent it to a young family from Montenegro.

Frankfurter Weg 7 was big enough for us anyway. Sophia lived in Bad Homburg, a 30-minute drive away, with her alcoholic friend, while Alim did pop art in Kuwait. I only stayed temporarily in Kastel until I could move back to my studio, which I was renting out.

One afternoon, I saw the renters of Paul-Ehrlich-Straße 4 loading a transporter with their belongings. Startled, I approached their 20-year old daughter and asked if they were moving out. "Yes. Your mother terminated the rental contract, effective immediately," she said. I looked at her with big eyes. I could not believe what she had just said. Suddenly, the entire family met me under the grape vine. They told me what had happened while my mother was watching us from the living room.

After they had finished, I excused myself and went back to Frankfurter Weg 7.

Upset, I confronted my mother in the living room. "Did you really terminate the rental contract?"

She looked at me as if it was not my business.

"How could you do that without informing us? Our family, especially you and Baba, depend on this rental income," I said, angrily.

"Oh please! My pension is enough for me!" she said. "You have no idea. I made the right decision. Last month they did not pay the rent on time, and this month they did not pay at all."

I looked at her, perplexed. "They just told me that the woman stayed in the intensive care unit for weeks, and that her husband was unemployed for a month, and that his new building contractor had not pay him yet. Did you know that?"

"Yes. But I am no welfare organization! I also have bills to pay!"

I shook my head. "I can't understand why you have no compassion for our renters. It's not that you couldn't survive six weeks without the rental income. Ending the contract was not a decision you should have done alone. It might not affect you that much, but Baba! His pension is almost zero. Why didn't you at least wait for him? You know he comes back next week. You could've made a reasonable decision together."

That was the moment she started shouting at me, "I knew it. You are a traitor. You've always been against me. You only take sides with our renters because they are foreigners from Montenegro and Muslims like you and your father!"

I looked at her furious eyes. "First, what you're saying about me is not true. Second, I talked about compassion and reason," I said even though I knew she would not listen to me.

She turned her back on me and ran out of the house.

Welcome back to my old life!

Friday, May 6, 2011

While I was in Fullerton, my Horizon scholarship was on hold. In May, it resumed, and I was looking forward to participating in further training and education.

The Horizon foundation invited me for a two-day training course in "Project Management" at their villa in Frankfurt. I was sitting with ten new scholarship holders at a long table in a meeting room, listening to the director's welcome speech. She announced, "I'm glad to present to you our new flyers and posters that will be distributed and presented nationwide." Next, she turned a page on the flip chart. I spotted three students on a poster. They kept the two females of the first version but changed the male in the center. *I was looking at a picture of me!* It had been taken at our training course in "Conflict Management" before I went to Fullerton. That day, I had been wearing a white dress shirt with bronze stripes.

The new scholarship holders looked at me with large eyes. "Wow, beautiful! Junis, this is you," they said. I did not know what to say. I was taken by surprise. I felt uncomfortable.

"Please, help distribute the flyers and poster. We've already sent them to 1,200 addresses nationwide, including all universities and institutions that educate teachers as well as many schools and the cooperation partners of the Horizon scholarship," the director said.

Next, she put a box on the front table and left the room. All the students got up and grabbed some flyers and posters, except *Faris,* who approached me.

"Did they ask you whether they could put you on these posters and flyers?" he asked.

"No. It was written somewhere in the contract that they could use pictures of me, but I thought they would ask me first. I just came from the U.S.A. I had no idea, damn," I said.

"Come on, I'd love to be on this poster. Be happy! You're a celebrity now."

"Yes. The prototype, exceptional immigrant who somehow managed in Germany," I said, pondering over it. *Being a "successful" immigrant wasn't something to be proud of, though. It should be normal, like in the U.S.A. Or could this poster change the image of immigrants in Germany and inspire other immigrant students to apply for the scholarship and attain their educational goals?*

Monday, May 16, 2011

The study regulations at Goethe University prescribed prospective teachers to complete an eight-week internship in a non-pedagogical institution to broaden their horizon. Since I was interested in policy-making processes, I applied for an internship at the "Ministry for Justice and Integration" (MJI). I was glad that I was accepted.

The week before the internship began, I bought a black and a light blue fitted dress shirt, black patent leather shoes, and a black leather belt in an upscale fashion boutique in the MTZ. I also went to the barber's to get a regular men's cut. After studying politics for almost four years, I was looking forward to my first experience in state politics.

I arrived at the central station at 9 a.m., 30 minutes prior to the registration appointment to make sure I would be on time. Leisurely, I crossed a park close by, heading toward the ministry. The morning sun was slowly getting warmer. Sunbeams gently touched my face, which was still gold-brown from sunny California. To my left, tall oak trees bordered the park, throwing a shadow on the sidewalk. To my right, fountains sprang water waist-high every five yards. A large field opened up behind the last well. I smiled at the lush green. *What a beautiful sight!*

Suddenly, I heard my shoes on the sidewalk, "tick-tock." They were stiff, like my dress shirt. *Did I look right?* I did not want to overdress, but I also did not want to look too casual. I wanted to look like a decent person. I was wearing dark blue jeans, a light blue dress shirt, black patent leather shoes, a black leather belt, and an anthracite suit coat.

The ministry stuck out with its natural stone facade and arched windows. Next to the security entrance door, I read on a golden plate, "State Penal System." The ministry for the integration of immigrants and the state penal system were located in the same building. It reminded me of my studies at CSUF on *Foucault*[67] and *how power served to control and punish the minority. The joint building fit with the mainstream media coverage*[68] *and public discourse that often portrayed immigrants as a burden if not menace to the democratic, German society.* My heart began to race. *Did I have a place here?*

I rang the bell. Shortly, a wide electronic door opened. I stepped into a shady, small entrance hall. An officer was sitting in a cabin in front of me, behind a security glass. "Your ID, please," he asked. I gave it to him. "Take a seat. You'll be called," he said. I sat down, nervous.

---

67 Paul-Michel Foucault (10/15/1926 - 06/25/1984), French philosopher, historian of ideas, social theorist, philologist, and literary critic
68 Informationen zur politischen Bildung (Heft 271). Neudruck 2009. *Vorurteile*. Bonn: SKN Druck und Verlag

After a while, the personnel manager came downstairs. She introduced herself and asked me to follow her. We took the spiral stairs to the fourth floor, where I was supposed to meet a member of the leading team. I read his name on the door sign, "Dr. Hoffmann." She entered his room. I followed her. She introduced me with my name and left.

Dr. Hoffmann came from his table to shake my hand. As we were facing each other, he looked me over from head to toe. I felt uneasy.

"Your name is interesting," he said.

"Pardon?" I said even though I understood him accurately. It was a defense I had developed after all the embarrassing interactions I had in Germany. *Was he aiming at my heritage? Why else would he make this categorical statement?* Usually, my anticipation was right. Yet, I could not know for sure and thus waited for his restatement.

"Sultan is an interesting name. Where are you originally from?"

Oh nice! The classic question I frequently received in Germany. I asked more clearly to find out what he was looking for, "What do you mean?"

"Where were you and your parents born? You look Mediterranean or Middle Eastern."

"My father was born in Iraq, I was, too, and my mother in Germany," I said, feeling how anger flamed up inside me. He forced me to instantly explain my background as if the reason for my non-German name and my non-whiteness were the most important thing about me. *Could he not wait until I felt like sharing a private part of me and of my family history?*

"Interesting. Your German is good. How come?" he asked, seriously.

I felt annoyed—unable to answer right away. *As if I naturally had to be uneducated because of my heritage.* "Well, I went to kindergarten, primary school, grammar school, and high school in Germany. And I've studied at Goethe University," I said before I noticed that I explained and defended myself, once again, even though it should have been unnecessary.

"Still, your German is really good. Many immigrants, especially Turks, stay here for years and they can hardly speak as fluently and accent-free as you do," he said.

I raised my eyebrows, weighed down. *When would we finally reach post-racial Germany?* I was speechless, while he brought forth a book that was lying on his antique table.

"Do you know this book?" he asked.

I said, "No."

"It was a bestseller in the U.S.A. It's about 9/11 and the terrorists who were on the plane. And it's about other terrorists who confess their activities in al-Qaeda and who left the organization and became normal people again. One even converted to Christianity. You should read it. It's really good," he told me while his eyes were still wide open.

Wasn't this the book Paul wanted me to read because I was a Muslim? Had Mr. Hoffmann anticipated that I was a Muslim? Did he want to educate and save me, like Paul? Or did he recommend that book to everyone he met?

I did not reply. I was sick of his attitude, *and he did not even notice.* Smiling, he shook my hand and wished me a good time in my internship while I just wanted to leave his office.

Wednesday, May 18, 2011

I approached my father in the kitchen around 10 p.m. He was just about to drink a cup of warm water, as usual before he would go to bed, when I asked him for some advice. He listened carefully while I told him about what had happened in the ministry.

"I'm sorry to hear that," he said. "You're in an exhausting position. You constantly have to prove that you're better than many people here think you are."

"Do I really have to prove this to people?" I looked at him with raised eyebrows.

"I know how you feel, but you need to be patient and work hard. Give it more time."

"And then what? Patience and hard work doesn't seem to change other peoples' attitudes. All my hard work and achievements of the last 20 years don't seem to matter in Germany.

I am still treated like a stranger. In the United States, I was almost always treated with love—regardless of my skin color, my name, or whatever superficial thing. I was accepted for who I was and respected for what I had achieved. What I experience here is simply wrong. I see it as clearly as never before. It's inhumane. It's intolerable. I'll absolutely not accept it."

"Look, I've met many politicians here as the chairman of the Council of Foreigners, and not only a few had prejudices against me. But in the course of time, even some of the tough ones changed their attitude since they saw that I wasn't primitive, uncultured, and lazy. It's not that we all became friends, but we can work together today."

"But I'm sick of their power games. I bow out. They can think of me whatever they want," I said. "I will not prove anything to them anymore because integration is not a one-way street. It's about mutual respect and meeting others halfway. Look, I did what I could, and still, I've remained a stranger. Why? Am I a complete failure? If so-called 'successful' immigrants like me have difficulties finding acceptance in the mainstream society, how shall immigrants with low socio-economic status ever be integrated? Is this really what we can call the developed world?"

My father looked at me, taken aback. "You've always weighed your options carefully before you made a decision. This internship is a good chance for your career. Don't lose it because of some idiots. But if you do, you should know why and whether it's worth it.

I nodded. "I know what principles I stand for."

He put his hand on my shoulder. "I appreciate that you come and ask your old man about what he thinks. You're a young man. I have been learning from you in the last few years. You know, whatever you decide, I stand behind you," he said.

That moment I knew I would turn my back on the so-called Ministry for Justice and Integration. I slowly calmed down, and yet I knew that what I would do would not be easy.

Thursday, May 19, 2011

At 8 a.m. I entered the personnel manager's office to give her my termination letter. She looked at me with large eyes. I told her that the letter contained an explanation. Since she insisted that she wanted to talk with me in person, I commented on what I had written down.

1. The "welcoming" by Dr. Hoffmann was marked by negative prejudices. I am disappointed that a leading member of the Ministry for Justice and Integration has such a biased, disrespectful attitude toward a particular group of immigrants.
2. Scientific work was unwanted. I intended to do this internship to gain and create more knowledge of the Hessian integration efforts. Indeed, I was asked to measure the integration projects

in quantitative and qualitative terms from 1999 onward. To do that properly, I would have had to request data sets from the Ministry for Social Affairs, which initiated integrations projects from 1999 to 2009 under the CDU before the FDP[69] took over the MJI and became responsible for integration. When I asked my superior for permission to make that request, I was told, however, that such a detailed data analysis was unnecessary since it was about showing numbers that put the current ruling party (FDP) in a good light. These cover-up tactics are untold.

3. Independent work was unwanted due to the coercion of promoting a party political agenda. More precisely, I was also asked to investigate the immigration policies of Canada and Australia to develop a similar, point-based concept for German immigration policies. This intended concept belongs to the political agenda of the FDP and is in the best scenario market-oriented but not human-rights-oriented. Regardless of the fact that I do not belong to any political party and that I do not want to promote any party political agenda, I can't identify with this concept because I believe in the humanitarian ideals.

---

[69] Free Democratic Party, liberal and classical liberal political party in Germany

In the end, she told me that she understood my decision.

"I'll also quit my job when I go on maternity leave. I've got a Polish migration background, and I frequently experience it in my everyday work, too," she said.

Her dark hair and her name on the nametag must have affected her in similar ways.

"Ius sanguinis, the right of blood still governs Germany," she said.

I got up, shook her hand, and left the ministry.

End of May 2011: diary entry

I'm sitting in the basement at our old dining table. It's midnight. The curtains are closed. I just crossed out the internship from my calendar on the wall. I have arrived in Germany, and it's still the same crap. I am still a stranger in Germany.

My parents are upstairs. I can hear their unending shouting about their financial problems …

I wonder, what shall I do now? WHAT SHALL I DO NOW?

VII. Liederbach

June 2011-November 2011

"Goodbye"

Sunday, June 26, 2011

I WAS LOOKING FORWARD TO moving back to my studio in Liederbach, *my old refuge*. When I opened the apartment door, a feeling of relief overcame me. I deeply breathed in, aware that I needed peace even more than in January 2009. Being back in Germany burdened me much more than I had expected. Old traumas, emotional flashbacks, and a reversed culture shock almost overwhelmed me. I fled from those negative thoughts and emotions into a work-mode. My final state exams were coming up, and I set myself the goal to achieve excellent grades. *The university degree was my ticket for a better future,* I still believed.

Monday, August 1, 2011

After school, I stopped by in Frankfurter Weg 7 to congratulate my parents for their 48th wedding anniversary. However, I only found my father. He was sitting in the kitchen, glaring at the table. He raised his head and stared at me as if the world would end today. "I quarreled with your mother. She ran away," he said. I looked at him, wordless and helpless. *In all these years, dozens of family meetings, family therapy, and constant efforts to understand and accommodate each other did not bring peace. Somehow, fighting always came back to us—tearing us apart.*

Tuesday, August 23, 2011: diary entry

My mother moved out on August 1. She has been living with Onkel Walter since then. She hasn't contacted me so far, and I'm afraid to call her. I don't know what to say. I'm afraid she has abandoned us for good. She has never run away for such a long time.

This afternoon, my father showed me a letter addressed to my mother. In the letter, his lawyer wrote that my father bemoaned her decision, but that he also accepted it. Furthermore, his lawyer proposed a meeting with her lawyer and her to clarify the questions of separation.

Monday, August 29, 2011: diary entry

This morning, two days before my 25th birthday, my father sued my mother for divorce. It's not the first time my parents have taken legal steps to separate. Since my father had come to Germany, my mother repeatedly contacted a women's aid organization and lawyers to get advice on the question of separation. Each time she changed her mind, though. I often wondered why she came back to us, even if I have never dared to ask her. It wasn't that I didn't want her to live with us, but everyone knew that she felt very unhappy with us. Maybe she just loved us in an egotistic way.

Maybe we all didn't love each other as much as we should have to live happily and peacefully together. Maybe cultural differences were only an excuse for our human failures. Whatever it was, all I know is that our struggles throughout the years, while trying to keep us together despite our painful conflicts, were in vain. Now, all hope is gone and written law will decide how we will be divided. I wonder, what is the lesson to learn?

SUNDAY, SEPTEMBER 4, 2011, MIDNIGHT: DIARY ENTRY

I'm sitting at my table. My white laptop screen illuminates my tense face while the dark night surrounds me. I'm trying to catch my wild thoughts and emotions. I'm trying to understand. I lost my parents, my siblings, my childhood, a central part of me. None of my siblings call me anymore. They don't want to talk about the family. I feel so lonely, so sad.

THURSDAY, SEPTEMBER 22, 2011: DIARY ENTRY

My father will go back to Iraq next week for an indefinite time. He wants to secure our property rights in Mosul. His lawyer told him that it would be difficult to get a share of the property in Kastel even though my father has invested about USD 300,000 over the years (mostly money from Iraq) to renovate

Paul-Ehrlich-Straße 4 and build Frankfurter Weg 7. However, my mother refuses to split the ownership in Kastel because Onkel Walter advises her so.

Today, I told my father that he shouldn't stress himself out for property issues since keeping up our relationships was much more important in this tough time. But he is obsessed with the idea that he will die soon and that he has to leave behind some secured property for us. He said, "Maybe you're too young, but you'll understand when you're old, when you have children and when suddenly everything you've built up for them over the years goes out the window for no just reason." I could not say a word. I understood his position as well.

I wonder what would have happened if we had never come to Germany—a place where differences have often been viewed as a threat for the so-called Leitkultur[70]. Maybe my parents would still be together. They didn't rip each other and our family apart in Iraq. Maybe my mother wouldn't have felt ashamed for who we are in Germany—a visible "ethnic" minority, the often alleged inferior and vulnerable "other."

If I had the money, I would take the next plane to California.

Tuesday, September 26, 2011: diary entry

Ya Allah, I haven't prayed for your help for some time, but please, if you can, help me. What shall I do without a family?

---

70 German, means "guiding culture"

Tuesday, November 7, 2011

It was already dark when I stopped by at Frankfurter Weg 7 to check how Mamun was doing. To my surprise, I saw my mother sitting in the living room. I had not seen her for months, and I still did not know how to approach her. *Did she move back because my father stayed in Iraq?* We looked at each other. "Hi," I said briefly and went to the kitchen to take a breath and think about how to behave. But I had no idea. Nervous, I opened the blue magazine that was lying on the table.

Suddenly, my mother approached me from behind. "The magazine lists the prices for solar panels. I want to buy some for Amtal," she said.

"Okay," I said, wondering how she could talk as if nothing had happened.

"Or maybe I'll buy a studio. You could help me find a good investment," she said.

I put down the magazine and decided to speak up. "No, I won't help you investing your money. If I may remind you, you deny us a share of what we built up together."

"We?" she said with large eyes. "I had to work day and night, not you or your father."

"That's not true. We all paid the price. We renovated, built, and maintained the houses together. We children helped as much as possible. And Baba often worked double shifts and brought thousands of dollars from Mosul throughout the years. And now, you simply want to kick us out of the house as if we had no rights whatsoever."

"Your father told you this stupid stuff. It's a lie."

"I wish it was," I paused. "I still can't understand why you and Baba can't split your finances like adults. We wanted to talk with you about it as a family, but you ran to Amtal."

"I ran away because he held a knife to himself on August 1 and threatened to commit suicide if I didn't agree to his offer. You weren't there," she shouted.

"No, I wasn't, and either Baba or you are lying about August 1. He showed me his affidavit in which he stated that none of all that happened. Either way, I can't understand you. He proposed that you keep one house and write the other one in the name of all children. Why couldn't you agree on that?"

She came toward me. "Because I can't trust you. You have always betrayed me. My own children have always been on their father's side."

Her words cut like an old knife. "We have not always betrayed you. We tried to be on the side of who was right, not because we wanted but because you and Baba forced us. And if we didn't take sides or the wrong side, you blamed or ignored us," I paused. "Do you know how painful it is to hear these sweeping accusations after all the years?"

"In my entire life, I was suppressed by my family and not allowed to be who I am. The houses in Kastel are my only security for the future. You'll not care for me once one house is in your names because your father has drummed into you that you cannot count on me or anyone in Germany because you are foreigners here and not accepted."

"Suppressed? How? When? I often went to church with you, also as a Muslim. We celebrated Christmas and Easter bigger than anything. You were free to be who you are, do what you want, and go where you want. We were not. And as regards Germany, discrimination was not Baba's invention but part of my experience here. Why don't you finally show some understanding?"

"Yeah, the Germans are always the bad guys, right? I have no bad conscience as a mother. I bought you food and clothes. I worked only for you. Still, my own children were strangers to me. They grew up with their father's culture and religion."

"They? Who are we in your eyes?"

I waited for an answer, but I didn't receive any. "I did not say all Germans are bad. I spent almost all my life in Germany. I enjoyed a good education here, and I also had good times with some good friends here. And if I may remind you, you raised us as well."

"And you still became a Muslim. You decided against me and for your father."

Tears filled my eyes. "This doesn't make sense. I told you many times. I did not decide against you. I made a religious decision for myself. I respected your faith and always will. All I expected from you was that you respect me as a human being with equal rights."

"I will never accept Islam. Islam lacks basic human principles."

Even though she had not told me all these words for the first time, I once again felt deeply hurt. "So are we all incomplete, inferior creatures, who are 'on the wrong side'?" I asked.

She took the book by Alice Schwarzer. Searching for a page, she said, "I can quote it. Islam says that a woman's witness reports doesn't count as much as a man's witness reports."

"Please! How does this relate to our family? Did we ever treat you like that?" I asked, but I did not receive an answer.

I packed my bag and, without looking back, left the house.

As I was walking away, she came to the garden fence. "Junis, you don't say goodbye?"

I looked over my shoulder and saw her waiting in the distance.

"Goodbye," I said quietly, not for the sake of courtesy, but because I meant it.

Epilogue

"A sense of warmth"

Friday, November 11, 2011

THE NEWS ANCHOR ANNOUNCED, "ACCORDING to the German federal bar, the 36-year-old Beate Zschäpe, who is a member of the neo-Nazi group 'National Socialist Underground' and who burned down her apartment in Zwickau on November 4, is connected to the murdering of a police officer and the serial murdering of nine immigrants, including five Kurdish, three Turkish, and one Greek Kebab store owners between 2000 and 2006.

He already assumed in 2006 that the murders had been conducted by neo-Nazis. *Chronic immigrant-bashing in the mainstream media had set the perfect atmosphere for neo-Nazis to operate.* Accordingly, even German officials wrongly accused the victims' relatives of having mafia businesses and thus being responsible for the murders. The hasty accusations had never been about solving the cases, he sensed, but about branding immigrants as evil. To make things worse, the murders were even observed by undercover agents and covered up by the Federal Office for the Protection of the Constitution until *Beate Zschäpe* burned down her house and parts of the truth had to be revealed to the manipulated, fear-conditioned public.

The years-long propaganda against immigrants left deep scars on his heart and on his arm. They hurt on countless days, but on this day, he felt perfectly lonely and helpless—abandoned by his last and inherent confidants: his family, the most trusted people in his life.

He turned off the television to go out for a walk. *Maybe nature could calm him down,* he thought. Yet, nature was already half dead. Fall had taken its course. The trees behind the parking lot faced him as leafless, fossilized skeletons. Struggle-weary, he bought cigarettes from the vending machine even though he had quit smoking. He did not care about his physical health anymore. His mental state was a devastated, contaminated battlefield. Thinking about his mother's last words, he lit a cigarette and inhaled the warm smoke.

Full of toxic shame, he started to walk through Liederbach. A kindergarten teacher saw him approaching. Tears were rolling down his face. She stared at him for a second before she moved inside the building. Demoralized by other people's callousness, he kept walking until, almost exhausted, he reached a field. Staring at brown, lifeless soil, total despair overcame him. *How could he live without his family? Without anyone?*

Hopeless, he slowly walked back to his apartment. He opened his laptop. *Angelo Milli's*[71] "Requiem" resumed. Piano tones and dramatic strings heralded the end. He stepped onto his balcony. The sky was clear for the first time in weeks. *How blue and beautiful,* he thought. Cold wind blew gently in his face while doves escaped to the heavens, but he was too weak to hold his body any longer. He went down on the cold concrete. His heart was pounding painfully. His spirit was flying away. *His life was meaningless because he was all alone. He might*

---

71 born 05/27/1975 in Venezuela, composer

as well be dead, he thought. *But would he dare to commit the biggest, irrevocable sin?*

The carpet cutter in the shoebox would do a deep cut! How long would it take to lose consciousness when he slashed his wrists? Would he finally feel relieved? What would his parents do when they found out? Would they stand together? Or blame each other? It did not matter to him anymore. He was determined to get the knife from underneath the kitchen sink.

All of a sudden, a sense of warmth surrounded him—as if someone was there and embraced him, as if this someone knew every thought he had and felt his inmost pain, as if this someone bled with him without complaint, as if this someone waited patiently, as if this someone asked him if he was truly ready to give up the chance of life, as if this someone promised that life had something good waiting for him. *Would he stand up one more time?*

Pictures ran through his mind like flashes: dropping bombs, a burning city, machine gun fire, dead people on the street, his father left behind at the gate, injured asylum seekers, his mother beating him, his neighbors shouting at him, a skinhead persecuting him, mass brawls at school, Marcus turning away from him, his mother turning away from him, his father dead still on a hospital bed, cutting himself, his brothers-in-law turning away from him, Ceylin turning away from him, his KO loss, his sister burning her arms, his parents fighting, his grandmother dead on a hospital bed, Dr. Hoffmann staring at him. *What should he do with his cursed life?* He wanted to throw it away.

But then, other pictures came to his mind: his mother looking after him while he seesawed in the garden, his father carrying him on his shoulders in the swimming pool, his family coming together around the Christmas tree, Oma Erika hugging him, his siblings kissing him on his birthday, Marcus and Dominik laughing with him, marching with the Kasteler band while people are clapping their hands, watching Martin Luther King Jr. speaking about his dream, Piero giving him his hand, Ceylin stroking him, winning a comeback-fight, Tom putting his hand on his shoulder, driving along the Pacific coast, singing and dancing with people from all around the world.

Tears streamed down his face. He was trembling. *Could he throw away these precious people? Could he throw away himself? What was the good thing that waited for him?* Could he possibly not feel lonely and worthless in the future? If there was the slightest chance for togetherness and happiness, would he seize it? If there was the slightest chance to be himself and develop himself as he chose, would he seize it? If there was the slightest chance for freedom and peace, would he seize it? Would he seize the chance of life? Would he look and work for his dreams with all his heart and with his entire mind, every day, without excuses? Could he keep the faith despite the struggles? Could he live a meaningful life?

Suddenly, the idea evolved in his mind. *The first thing he would have to do to not only survive, but heal, was to write everything down. Maybe he would understand himself better by putting it all on paper.* Maybe he would grasp the thoughts and emotions that have driven him. Maybe he would triumph over the fears of being separated from others and from himself. Maybe he would develop the courage to fully love himself. Maybe he would forgive himself for his destructive behaviors. *Maybe he would also develop more understanding for people.* Maybe he would develop the courage to fully love all people and forgive also those who are difficult to love for their destructive behaviors.

Maybe he could even use his story and help create something good for people. Maybe his story could help people deal with their fears and despairs. Maybe it could encourage people to love themselves and other people. Maybe it could help people forgive themselves and other people. Maybe it could make people turn to each other. Maybe it could help people build deep connections to each other. Maybe it could tear down some old walls and help build something new, something good. Maybe it could somehow unite East and West, old and young, men and women—humanity.

This was the only way his life made sense to him. It had never been about Junis Sultan but about living, sharing, and encouraging the human experience: the needs for bonding and freedom, the struggles for happiness and peace, and the connecting and liberating powers of love.

Made in the USA
Columbia, SC
13 October 2017